BLACK JESUS,
WHITE JESUS

BLACK JESUS, WHITE JESUS
THE SEARCH FOR A COLORLESS CHRIST

BY CHRISTOPHER KING

XULON PRESS

Xulon Press Elite
2301 Lucien Way #415
Maitland, FL 32751
407.339.4217
www.xulonpress.com

Unless otherwise indicated, Scripture quotations taken from the New King James
Version (NKJV). Copyright © 1982 by Thomas Nelson, Inc. Used by permission. All
rights reserved.

Printed in the United States of America.

ISBN: 9781545613313

DEDICATION

I dedicate *Black Jesus, White Jesus* to my loving family. To my wife—Ebony. You have always been my cheerleader. My support system and my helper. God has truly answered my prayers with you. To my daughters—Morgan, Kristyn, and Kree. There is no father on earth more proud of his children. I love you dearly. To my brothers—Marvin and Tony. Each struggle has been worth it. I can't imagine what life would have been without you guys by my side. To Nana. I'm convinced you are an angel.

To my friends and colleagues who supported me during this process. I love you and thank God for each of you.

TABLE OF CONTENTS

INTRODUCTION

My father is a country (rural) boy at heart. After dedicating more than thirty years of his life to his professional pharmaceutical career in Houston's big city, he retired, quickly packing his bags for Mississippi's country living. Now, he spends his time in the fields, happily raising his herd of cattle. Like I said before, my father is a country boy. And I can't think of a place more country than Mississippi. To a young city boy like myself, Mississippi's social scene is much slower paced than my hometown—Houston, Texas. And while I have enjoyed quite a few summer vacations in Mississippi as a child, I would still be hard pressed to categorize it as one of my favorite places.

Historically, Mississippi has been widely known for its overt racism toward blacks and other minority groups. Dating back to slavery, Mississippi was a hotbed for black oppression and discrimination. While the rest of the country may have shifted to more covert and systematic methods of racism, Mississippi has proudly held true to its history. Sad to say, the stench of such practices still corrodes the air of the state's culture. Unfortunately, this culture has also planted itself within the church.

During summer 2015, as my father sat in his home enjoying a nice break from tending to his cattle, a nice, well-dressed white man appeared at his door. When my father answered, the man appeared to be confused.

Looking around as if he were expecting someone else to answer the door, he politely asked, "Excuse me. Are you the owner of this home?"

After retirement, my father built a beautiful home and ranch on more than 150 acres of land. In defense of the stranger, such homes (and land) are not typically owned by blacks in this area. Not only was this a sizable home sitting on acres of land, it was painted white. It is an unwritten, but often spoken rule of the rural black community there, that blacks are not to paint their house white as this is seen as disrespectful to whites in the area. So, this stranger approaches a large white house, resting on more than 150 acres of land; and a black man opens the door. If I were him, I might have thought he was the help as well. Nevertheless, my father kindly obliged his guest.

"Yes. I am the owner," he said.

"Well, I am the new pastor of the church down the road," the man said, introducing himself. "And I wanted to come by and invite you to worship with us this Sunday."

I am not sure if he truly expected my father to worship with them or not. But it was obvious my father didn't take the invitation too seriously.

With a slight chuckle, my father responded, "Sir, I am very sure you're not from around here. But you don't want me to come to your church. Because if I do, you won't be the pastor anymore. I thank you for stopping by. God bless you." He then politely closed the door.

My father was operating from the cultural understanding that there are many things we are now permitted to do alongside our white brothers and sisters. We can shop with them, eat and go to school with them. But, in no way, are we to worship with them. This understanding is not only reserved for the rural areas in Mississippi, but can be witnessed all over the United States and in other parts of the world. It is a mindset that has led to the emergence of a variety of church categories—black church, white church, Hispanic church, etc. It has created racial lines of demarcation within an institution that was never intended to be divided. These lines are the basis of this book.

As a child, I grew up in the black Baptist church. When I say I grew up in the church, I literally mean, I grew up in the church. On Sunday, I woke up early to attend Sunday school, and then went to a morning church service. After service, we often ate dinner with our church community, only to return later to an evening service. On Monday, my brothers and I had church activities for various auxiliary ministries we were a part of. On Tuesday, we went to a mid-week Bible study service. Many churches have their mid-week service on Wednesday. But, for reasons unknown to me, our church chose to have it on Tuesday. So, on Wednesday, we had the day off. Thursday was choir rehearsal, while Friday often included additional church activities for children. Saturday was often another off day. And then on Sunday morning, we started the process all over again. So, when I say I lived at the church, you can under-stand I spent most of my childhood at church. And none of my parents were ministers. This is all because my mother wanted to raise us in a God-fearing home. But when I looked around at my church family, there was one glaring similarity. They all looked like me.

Martin Luther King, Jr., once referred to Sundays at 11a.m. as the most segregated hour in America.[1] When I was a young boy, like many others, I experienced this same segregation. As a black family, we worshipped with other black families and never considered worshipping anywhere else. The thought of worshipping with other cultures wasn't overtly discouraged. However, now I am older and have had a few more experiences, I can say the messages I received, either directly or indirectly, perpetuated such segregation.

One day, as a young boy, I asked my mother why we didn't go to church with any white people. Hearing this question, my mother replied, "Well, our music is different than theirs and we just have different preferences." Now, let me put into context the paradigm from which my mother saw things. My mother grew up in Vicksburg, Mississippi, in the mid-1940s. This was a time when racial tensions in the south were at their peak. To simply say there was racial injustice doesn't truly speak to the times, and would be nothing more than a severe understatement. There were killings and church bombings. Segregation and racism made being black a life-threatening "job." So, as a child, there were times I could see she hadn't quite been healed of her distrust of white America. So, because of "differences in worship style," we were discouraged from worshipping with other cultures. As we will explore later in this book, this statement does not have to be true.

Another way the limitations were perpetuated was through the color (or ethnicity) debate of Jesus. Every February during Black History month, I was sure to hear a sermon on the influence of black people in the Bible, only to be capped off with the emotionally charged statement that Jesus was black, as they referenced particular scriptures in Daniel (chapters 7 and 10). While these messages ignited black Christians with a sense of pride, it also served as a platform for more segregation and even more questions. If Jesus is black, why do I see so many pictures of this white guy? If Jesus is black, do white people know? If we are worshipping Black Jesus, who are they worshipping, White Jesus? If this is the case, which one is right? Who wins? As a young boy, these were the questions that arose in my mind all while "White Jesus" seemed to become more unavailable and equally undesirable. Although I continued my prideful allegiance to "Black Jesus," many years later, I would make an about-face and attempt to quench a rising thirst for his counterpart.

In fall 1995, I escaped the challenges of my impoverished youth and attended college at Drake University in Des Moines, Iowa. Although Drake initially began in the mid-1800s as a religious institution, in 1995, it possessed the character of most colleges across the country — an exciting social scene, but popularized by its emphasis on academic excellence with little emphasis on faith and spirituality. But by now, my spiritual paradigm had already been established by the black Baptist church and the black culture I had grown up in. Upon my arrival on campus, there was one thing that was clear. There weren't very many black people. It was a complete culture shock. I instantly came from an environment where everyone in my neighborhood, at my school, at the grocery store and at church looked exactly like me. They talked, danced and most of all, struggled like me. But now, I was one of few. I was merely a brown face in what seemed to be a sea of white.

As I saw it, everyone else's life seemed so less complicated. Everyone appeared to have been exposed to a world I only witnessed in movies and read about in books. Their lives seemed clean and well-structured. Many of them appeared well-travelled and affluent. Unlike me, many of the people I met were from a well-to-do family consisting of both parents living in the household. Their parents dropped them off at school, helped them decorate their dorm rooms, kissed them goodbye and wished them good luck for the year. I arrived on campus with my older brother, with barely enough money to buy dinner that evening. At the time, everything about my life represented struggle and hardship. Everyone else's life looked so much more appealing than mine. However, I continued to decorate my dorm room with décor to insist to the world that I was proud to be black. But the truth is, at that time, I wasn't too sure if I was. As a matter of fact, this was the reality I faced as I interacted with other students on campus.

Before long, there would be a mounting frustration and anger that I was unprepared to overcome. At that point, the divide between white and black became bigger for me. To be more specific, the color line was not merely a comparison between two competing cultures; but became a comparison between two deities—"Black Jesus" and "White Jesus." While I still possessed some level of respect for Black Jesus, it became frustratingly obvious that White Jesus loved his people more than Black Jesus. So, based on what I saw and was currently experiencing, White Jesus was winning. And I wanted to be a part of the winning team.

Going forward, we will examine my pursuit of White Jesus while trying to maintain my credibility and loyalty to Black Jesus and his people. We will explore my spiritual findings as I struggled to be progressive but continued to relate to where I had come from. We will examine the spiritual color line that is perpetuated in today's mainstream churches. In this examination, we will see that the color line within the Christian church is self-imposed. Not only is it self-imposed, but it relegates us all — black, white, Hispanic, etc. — to the very places we are attempting to avoid. Now as we embark upon this journey, let me briefly tell you what this book is not.

For starters, this is not a book that is intended to bash or overly criticize a particular culture (black or white) or the Church. It is merely an examination of several of my experiences, meant to highlight the damaging effects that the self-imposed spiritual color line has caused and illustrate places of convergence for all of God's people. This book is also intended to prayerfully lead readers to an authentic experience with Him, with the understanding that this experience washes away any painful residue that the color line has left on our lives. This book ultimately is intended to serve as a guide for how the color line is to be permanently washed away by the Holy Spirit within the Church and thus, across the nation and the world. This is not just a call for the washing away of the color line. This book is a prophetic utterance through His Holy Spirit that the color line will be washed away and God will freely reign among His people. I pray the words on each page are received in the Spirit in which they are written and quicken your spirit. I pray your heart can be opened and you can experience and become a willing participant in what the Holy Spirit is doing among the various cultures and generations across the land. In Jesus' name, Amen.

PART 1 – THE STRUGGLE

GOD IN THE MIDST OF OUR CIRCUMSTANCES

"In Jesus' name. Amen," the pastor announced to the congregation, indicating the conclusion of his prayer and the culmination of the church service.

I must admit, those were the only words I heard, as I wasn't paying much attention to the prayer. Like most times, this prayer seemed to last an eternity. As a young boy, I habitually found myself timing the prayers during the church service. Every time someone prayed, I would glance down at my prized Mickey Mouse watch and time how long it took them to say what they had to say. There was one time a prayer literally lasted for more than fifteen minutes. The people praying thanked God for everything from the sun that rises and sets at the end of the day to the silkworm that produces silk. Many times, it seemed as if they were simply repeating themselves, as they did everything in their power to extend their prayer. But even if their prayers were only thirty seconds, I am sure it would not have met my standard for an appropriate prayer length. For a young boy, even the shortest prayer would have been too long. And this time was no different. So as the final words escaped the pastor's lips that evening, once again, I was overjoyed because his prayer and the service were finally over.

My mother must have been just as excited, because before he put the final syllable on his last word, it seemed as if she jetted from her usual position in the choir stand and ran out the front door of the church. The choir stand was the area directly behind the main stage (or the pastor's pulpit), where the choir would sit during service, visible to the entire congregation. Access to the choir stand required one to enter through a back door, typically hidden from the general population. Usually after service, my mother could be found talking and fellowshipping with her church friends for what easily seemed like hours well after the service was over. There were several times we were the last to leave the church parking lot, as her friends would laugh and talk throughout the night. However, there was something particularly different after this service. She was on a mission and if I didn't want to get left at church, I would need to hurry as well. Matching her urgency, I quickly met her and my brothers outside the worship sanctuary in the church foyer.

I often joke and tell people that as a young boy, I lived at church. We went to church on Mondays, Tuesdays, Thursdays and on Fridays. And on Sundays, we often had multiple services we would attend. There were only two days out of the week we didn't go to church. So now, you can understand why I often say as a young boy, I lived at church.

This particular evening, we were attending our usual midweek worship service that didn't end until late in the night. Beginning promptly at 7pm, the service ended approximately at 10:30. That's three-and-a-half hours. Even in today's standards, that's a long time. So to a child (and on a school night), that was much later than desired. But that wasn't the reason for my mother's haste. It wasn't until we finally were inside the car that I understood the need for her urgency.

"Ma, why are we running?" I inquired.

"Boy, just get in the car," she exclaimed. My mother often referred to us simply as *boy,* because she seldom remembered which son she was talking to.

4

It was as if she forgot our names. So rather than say the wrong name, she just said *boy*. I guess that's something that happens when you have three boys.

"Come on. Just hurry up, Chris," my older brother added, as he opened the car door and escorted me into the back seat of our white 1976 Buick Riviera. Once we were in the car, the details of our emergency became a little clearer to me.

"There's a big storm coming. So we have to go," my mother explained.

Texas storms have been known to be quite fierce. And this one was expected to be a torrential downpour. Also, the city of Houston was located at sea level (and in some places, below sea level), with a very poor drainage system. So, there were constant issues with flooding. At the time, we lived approximately thirty-five minutes away from the church.

The main reason my mother was in such a hurry was because we all had very little confidence in our ten-year-old car making the journey in such conditions. Our car was the exact definition of a hoopty (or a lemon). In urban terminology, a hoopty was a raggedy, or broken down car. While the outside emblem suggested it was a Buick Riviera, I am sure along the way it acquired a few foreign car parts. It drove like a tank and looked like it had been in several battles. If it started on the first crank, we considered it a miracle, as it would often stall at a stoplight of its choosing. It seemed to possess its own mind and will, and we were always at its mercy. This was our car. Over its ten years, it had obviously taken a beating.

Not only were we insecure in our car's ability to successfully make the trip under such conditions, but we also knew that our windshield wiper system was broken. Up until that point, we had always done a fairly good job of making sure that the weather was sunny with clear skies whenever we needed to drive. And if ever we did get caught in rain, it was typically a light drizzle. But this night would be different. As quickly as we rushed to beat the storm, our efforts were in vain. Within ten minutes of our journey, the skies opened on the city and drowned our car in what seemed to be a monsoon. Instantly, we found ourselves in the midst of one of the fiercest storms I had witnessed since Hurricane Alicia in 1983. For those unaware, Hurricane Alicia was (and still is) considered one of the most devastating storms to hit the Texas coast. And although this storm had not reached hurricane status, it definitely brought to mind similar fears and experiences encountered just a few years prior.

The rain came down in sheets. Thunder rolled and streaks of lightning lit up the darkened night sky. The winds were so strong, I could often feel our car shake from the force. My mother's ability to see the road was almost completely blocked by the downpour that engulfed us. Fear overcame us as our car unpredictably hydroplaned over the slick streets. And the fact that the car's windshield wipers didn't work only added a level of drama we would have rather done without.

"JESUS!" my mother shouted. "Lord, please help us get home," she continued praying aloud.

Although we were all glad she had the confidence to pray, we weren't as certain of how successful her prayers would be this night. At the time, we had two options. One: pull over to the side of the road and wait until the storm passed over. Or two: brave it out and press on toward our Southwest Houston apartment home. Given the area was known to flood at the slightest precipitation, waiting on the side of the road would have placed us in more danger, as our car would have become a 3,000-pound boat. The only difference was, our car couldn't float. Either option seemed destined to produce the same catastrophic result. But with God's help, my mother's ingenuity, and some good old-fashioned elbow grease from my older brother, we braved the storm and pressed our way home.

At my mother's direction, Marvin—my older brother— grabbed an old wire coat hanger resting on the car's floor. Along with being a piece of junk, our car was often filled with junk. With so many activities, we were always on the go. After school, there was rarely enough time to travel home to change clothes. So we often scarfed down McDonalds hamburgers and changed clothes in the car as we darted to our church activities during the week. So, to us, an old coat hanger sitting in the car was not a coincidence. It was merely a result of us not removing it after changing clothes in the car. So, grabbing the wire coat hanger, my brother untwisted it until it was completely straightened, looking more like a wire stick than its previous form. He then re-twisted it to form a small loop on one end, shaping it into a makeshift lasso.

As we crept through the partially flooded streets of Houston, Marvin (who was twelve years old at the time) let down the passenger side window. His face easily said more than his mouth would allow that night. At one moment, his frustrated face showed he was tired of being poor and struggling through life. In another instance, his expression seemed to indicate he would be perfectly okay if everything came to a devastating end that night. Unfortunately, my fear wouldn't allow me to feel sorry for him as I merely looked on, hoping that whatever he was challenged to do, he'd meet it with great success.

As he let down the window, water instantly rushed into the car, drenching all of us. From the sky. From the ground. It seemed as if the rain was pouring in from all directions. Coaching him every step of the way, my mother urged him to hook the loop of the wire contraption to the broken windshield wiper and manually clear the way. Marvin was much bigger in size than most kids. This often forced him to take on greater responsibilities and challenges than most children would've had to face. People often saw his size and mistook him to be much older, forgetting that he was merely a twelve-year-old child. And this was one of those times. Nevertheless, he went into action, sticking his upper body outside of the car to manually wipe the windshield with his makeshift windshield wiper lasso contraption.

Not letting up, the rain seemed to come down harder with every second. Every street we travelled on was now flooded, and the water seeped up through the floor of our car. Despite how bad the rain continued to fall, Marvin kept fighting the onslaught of water hitting his face. That night, he became our human guide as he moved the wire coat hanger contraption back and forth across the windshield. For the next twenty to thirty minutes, he continued to wipe the windshield, giving my mother an opportunity to bring us home.

"Thank you, Jesus," my mother said as we finally pulled into the driveway. The usual thirty-five minute journey took more than an hour and a half that night.

By now, Marvin was completely drenched from his efforts. We were all thankful we finally arrived safely at our destination. It was clearly one of the scariest moments I had experienced in the first eight years of my life. And clearly, one I would never forget.

Ironically, this episode was illustrative of my childhood. While on this particular night we battled a physical storm, there were many storms and struggles we'd undergo during my childhood. We experienced social storms. Cultural storms. Storms of personal loss and storms where our safety was often jeopardized. But most of all, it seemed as if we were constantly in a storm of shortage, as we often experienced financial hardships.

Through every storm, my mother could be heard crying out to God for assistance and deliverance. My mother was what some would consider "a praying woman." At any time of the day, she could be heard praying to God, especially during times of trouble. No matter the storm, my mother would pray. And there were many storms. This would be something I'd grow to appreciate.

However, as an eight-year-old boy, it confused me. It seemed every chance we had, we were at church, worshipping God. We rarely missed a church service. But no matter how often we went to church, we were often fighting for our lives and crying out to the same God to deliver us from whatever storm we were experiencing. And honestly, it seemed the one thing we did more than go to church was struggle. Every day of my childhood seemed like a struggle or a storm. Even at such a young age, I was able to conclude one thing for sure – I didn't like struggling as much as we did. But during all of our struggles, what I didn't understand was the point of going to church so much when all we were going to do was struggle. If we were going to struggle, why did I have to go to church? And if I went to church, why did I have to struggle? This question was often the basis for several of my unsuccessful pleas to my mother to pardon me from my church obligations. Nevertheless, we continued to go to church and struggle faithfully.

As a young boy, there was one piece of spiritual advice I couldn't help but remember. No matter what was going on in our lives, I learned that Jesus could deliver us from our struggles. "If ever you're in trouble or in a jam, just call on the name of Jesus," my mother would say. This was definitely something I saw her practice on a daily basis. "Jesus, Jesus, Jesus." There seemed to be a constant ring of "Jesus" throughout the house. When the rent was due and eviction notices piled up, she called on Jesus. When the electricity was disconnected... Jesus. And when she was diagnosed with cancer, Jesus was definitely called to be her helper. From the simple to the most complex of struggles and problems, Jesus was called to be there. But from my young perspective, if Jesus could deliver us from our struggles, why didn't he? For as many jams as we were in and as many times as she called his name, why were we still struggling?

At the time, my understanding of God was primarily as creator and judge. That is, God created everything and was sitting on high, judging everything I did. If I did things correctly according to the rules, good things would happen. The more God liked you, the more He blessed you. If you weren't on His good side, good things were fleeting, leaving you to a life of struggle and strife. So, since our family life was filled with struggle and many hardships, I could only reason that my family (my mother, brothers, and/or myself) weren't in God's good graces. And given that God created everything, He was also responsible for everything—including (especially) the storms and struggles of my life (so I thought). So as a young boy, my understanding was that God caused the storms in my life and would (and should) deliver me if and only if I met His standards. Therefore, instead of being "God in the midst of my circumstances," He became "the God who caused my circumstances."

This mindset is still a teaching that exists in many churches today. However, many try to dress it up by saying God created your storms to build your character and your faith. But this isn't accurate.

Just a side note (which may become another book in itself): God is not the creator of your storms. Yes, He allows us to go through them. But Scripture never says He creates them. Yes, your storms can be a result of, or influenced by, Satan. But most of our storms are a result of our disobedience, poor decisions, ignorance, etc. There's a major difference in God creating a storm versus Him allowing you to go through one created by the enemy, or self-inflicted.

But that's not the message conveyed in most churches. And it wasn't the message I heard in my upbringing. So, as I got older and experienced many more storms throughout my life, I continued to maintain my "Good God, Good Things" theology.

This theology would serve as the foundation for how I would see and experience God for much of my life. Unfortunately, it also aided in creating a disdain for a god I would at some point seek to replace. Again, it's a similar theology many in the Church still possess today.

DOES HEAVEN
HAVE A GHETTO?

I came home from school and saw a pile of flattened cardboard boxes spread out across the living room floor. Just like the other times, my mother simply commanded us to pack all of our things into the boxes. This was not a new occurrence. In fact, I became quite accustomed to the routine. Pack our belongings in boxes. Load them into the car. Move to another apartment only to wait for the next eviction notice and start the whole process over again. Like I said, this was a regular occurrence. We moved constantly. I can name at least seven different addresses I had as a kid, all on the same street. And that's not counting the other places we moved to. There were even times we moved next door to the place we were just evicted from. So, the moving process was nothing new to me and neither was the eviction process. Growing up in our home, either the electricity was being disconnected, we were being served with an eviction notice, or the rat infestation was so bad it forced us to move. On one occasion, my older brother beat a rat off of me as I lay asleep on the living room floor. As my mother used to say, "If it wasn't one thing, it was another." And although this had become the norm for our family, this move would be entirely different.

Unfortunately, I remember many details about this day, as it didn't have the best start. That morning, I had a particularly rough time at school. Only in the third grade, I had been through a day filled with what would be considered bullying in today's schools. But the sensitivity of such topics had not come about yet, so it was just a day in the life of an urban third grader. It was no secret. My family wasn't the wealthiest on the block.

In fact, years earlier I was struck by a drunk driver while riding my bike. When the paramedics came, and after I finally regained consciousness, I was more concerned the paramedics had cut my only pair of school pants than I was about the blood rushing from my face and mouth. At that time, I only had two pair of pants—school pants and church pants. Since they had cut my only pair of school pants to examine my injuries, I was only left with my navy-blue church pants. Going to school in church slacks was sure to send an invitation for some good old-fashioned ribbing by the neighborhood kids.

I am not sure if you are familiar with the inner workings of the minority public school system, but kids are cruel. There's a great deal of pressure to look your best. Oftentimes in inner city schools, students often act as if every day is a fashion show. Now, truth be told, most of the students there were not from affluent backgrounds. Now that I am older, I realize many of them were struggling just like me. But in the minority communities, there is a sense of pride. Even if you are struggling, you better not look like it. If you must, you spend your last dime looking like you are worth a million dollars. Even today, one can travel down any inner city street and see the same behavior. Well, this behavior is often perpetuated in the schools. And if there happens to be a person who does not look "the part," the other kids are determined to point it out. They go for blood. So even at a very young age, I was conditioned to be concerned with what other children would say about my clothes. And while three years had passed from the drunk driver incident and

I had a new pair of school pants, there were still aspects of my wardrobe that seemed to invite trouble — specifically, my shoes.

For as long as I can remember, I have been "hard" on shoes. My shoes would appear to wear out much faster than my brothers'. And while I am able to afford a nice pair of shoes now, as a child, my family didn't have that luxury. Just like my pants, I possessed two pairs of shoes. Yep, you guessed it — school shoes and church shoes. Just like my school pants, my school shoes often doubled as play shoes and "everything else" shoes. With so much activity, they were bound to need replacement at some time. Unfortunately, the time they needed replacement didn't coincide with my mother's ability to replace them. There was only one time throughout the year we were allowed to get new clothes and shoes, and that was the week before school began. And that wasn't guaranteed. She would often go shopping for new clothes, only to reserve them on layaway. Layaway was a system many stores established to reserve items you intended to buy, by making regular payments. You weren't allowed to take any of the items home until the items were paid in full, which in our case seldom happened. But, if your shoes wore out between that time and the next shoe date, you were often fresh out of luck. And on this particular day, my shoes had given up the fight.

As I participated in the daily relay races during recess, I heard a flapping sound as I ran. Every stride I made, there was the flap. Determined to beat the person I was racing against, I confidently continued. Step. Flap. Step. Flap. Step. Flap. All the way to the finish line. I won. But instead of experiencing the joys of victory, I felt the frustrations of embarrassment as the other kids laughed. The soles of my shoes were separating from the actual shoe. They laughed, saying my shoes were talking to me because the front of the shoe looked like a mouth. To be honest, that wasn't the part that embarrassed me. The embarrassing part was I knew there was a great chance I would continue to have those same "talking" shoes for the rest of the school year, because my mother really couldn't afford to get me any others. So, for me, the day didn't get off to the best start. And to come home from school and see the cardboard boxes sprawled across the floor was even further indication I wouldn't get a new pair of shoes anytime soon.

As I mentioned before, the moving process was normal for us. It was never our desire, but out of necessity. Given that we were often evicted for not being able to keep current with rent payments, the moves never seemed to come as a surprise to my mother. She always seemed to keep calm and create a plan to find another place to live. But this time was different. There was no plan and there was no other place to live. But we (my brothers and I) wouldn't find this out until later that night. As we did during the other moves, we packed the car with as many boxes and trash bags as could possibly fit. We were accustomed to making multiple trips to the new house to transport all of our belongings. The plan would often be that we took everything we could fit in the car, and my mother would arrange for someone to come with a truck to transport the furniture.

So up until this point, everything still felt quite normal. However, as we drove with boxes and garbage bags filled with our clothes and necessities, it was never quite clear where she was headed. It seemed like she drove all around town.

"Mama, where are we going?" I asked.

"Oh baby, we're just riding and enjoying the day," she replied.

But by now, the day was clearly drawing to a close and we had yet to arrive at our new place. Finally, when the sun went down, my mother slowly pulled the car into what appeared to be a nice, safe neighborhood and confirmed what I was suspecting.

"Okay y'all, I wasn't able to get us a new place yet. But we have everything we need right here. We have our clothes and we have each other. But most of all, we have love. And that's all we need. I really wish we had somewhere to stay, but we don't. And I want y'all to know I am sorry and I love you," she solemnly expressed.

I can't speak for my brothers but I really felt her pain. I felt she had been trying her best to provide us with the life she thought we deserved. The last thing she wanted was to see us experience sleeping in our car. In his typical diplomatic fashion, my older brother, simply said, "It's okay, Momma," as each of us began to nestle into whatever comfortable space we could find and prepared to make our home in our trusted Buick Riviera. Exhausted from the stress of it all, my mother said a simple prayer, expressed her love for us, and said good night.

From the outside, one could easily suggest my mother take us to a shelter. But to her, that signified defeat. You see, my mother was a very proud woman, and much of her pride rested in her ability and strength to be successful when all others doubted her. As a child, I witnessed countless times when the odds and others were against her. Despite how the circumstances looked, she always found a way to pull through. This became a staple of her identity. So for her to go to a shelter, the very image she created for herself and took pride in would be challenged. So, we simply stayed in our car.

The next few days required some major adjustments. In public, we maintained the image that everything was normal. But privately, we knew at the end of the day we would drive around to find a place to park and sleep. In the morning, we would wake up to bathe in the sinks of the cleanest local gas station restrooms we could find, before being dropped off at school. While our daily circumstances had clearly taken a turn for the worse, there were two things my mother would not let suffer—the strong focus on our education and schoolwork, and our commitment to church. We didn't have a stable place to live, but we were always to show our faces at the many church activities and worship services that took place.

I am not sure my mother continued to go because it gave us a place to stay other than the car for a few hours, or if her

---

spiritual commitment was really that strong. As for me, I appreciated the break from being confined to a crowded car, but my faith wasn't that strong. After all, I was just a young boy. I had experienced enough to question the very faith and God I was encouraged to believe in. In fact, at the wee age of eight, I was ready to throw in the towel with all of the church stuff. Besides, what kind of God would make us homeless? What had I done to Him? And while our bout with homelessness only lasted a little more than a week, it did enough damage to me to raise a lot of questions (with few answers).

DON'T LET THOSE WHITE BOYS BEAT YOU

As I mentioned earlier, my entire paradigm as a young boy was naturally based on the black cultural experience. Historically, the black cultural experience has been a competitive one. Since the beginning, black people have found themselves on the end of one struggle or another in America. We fought to survive the horrors of the Middle Passage. We fought for our freedom from slavery. We fought for civil rights, and we are still fighting today. Therefore, the black cultural experience doesn't *just* measure success by the outcome of the fight with white culture, but by the amount of fight that's within us. While this idea can be witnessed in many aspects of black culture, it is truly prevalent in sports.

The only time I really had any serious interaction with white people, or any other cultures, was in the competitive arenas of the basketball court or on the football field. No matter what the event or activity, if there were white people on the other side, I couldn't lose. Not that I was physically unable to lose; but more so, I wasn't allowed to lose. "Don't let those white boys beat you," was the mantra on every level and in most areas of my life.

Don't get me wrong. It wasn't a battle cry based on a disdain for white people. At least, it wasn't for me. I am sure for some, it may have been. But for most, I feel it was less about disdain for the other race (or culture) and more of a need to be seen as significant and relevant by the "competition." It's a statement saying, "I've struggled for so long to find significance within myself and a society that refuses to recognize any value within me, so I must fight for the significance I feel I deserve." It's perpetuated in so many areas of American society. Athletics. Education. In finance and entertainment. This idea is also exemplified throughout corporate America in what is often referred to as the "Black Tax." That is, as a black man, one must be twice as good as their white counterparts to be considered just as significant and relevant.

So, when parents, coaches, mentors, teachers, and other black leaders cried, "Don't let those white boys beat you," it was never a charge to incite hate toward the other. Rather, it was a statement implying white people didn't take us seriously, or value us. But when you beat them, they must acknowledge that you are serious, significant and just as good. I took it as a fight to prove that I belonged. And while I write from a black perspective, I am more than certain the reverse took place on the opposite sides of the field. So, it was often a call perpetuated on both sides—white and black. Whites were pushed to win to show that blacks didn't belong, and blacks were driven to win to show that we did.

This was evident during the 1995 Texas state high school basketball playoffs. It was my senior year and our team was coming off a banner year, winning the previous Class 5A Texas State Basketball Championship. We faced high expectations, and as this year's team captain and leading scorer, I had a lot to prove. The previous year, I received a glimpse of what victory and success felt like, and I wanted nothing more than to experience it for a second, consecutive year. Besides, it would be my last year donning the uniform of a Willowridge Eagle, and I wanted to go out with a bang. You see, my high school had a rich history of successful athletic teams. Football, basketball and track and field were all sports where we led the pack, and in many cases, we dominated. So, along with the desire to repeat that championship feeling, there was the tremendous pride to continue the winning tradition.

It was the first round of the playoffs and we were matched up against the Katy Tigers. Growing up, Katy High School was predominantly made up of an affluent white student population. Like us, Katy also had a rich tradition of winning. In fact, they were widely known for breeding athletes who literally looked like giants. There was a system at Katy High in which they seemed to produce some of the finest athletic specimens seen in any high school arena. Their football teams often crushed their opponents as if they were bugs. And their basketball teams were no different: pure giants with an insatiable appetite for winning.

Contrast that with our team of black players who also came from a winning pedigree, and you had the makings of an outstanding clash that would mean more than just who would advance to the next round of the playoffs. Each team would be representing their respective communities. Their people. Black versus white. A battle of epic proportions.

Before I stepped one foot onto the court, I may have had at least a dozen people give me the same pre-game pep talk. "Don't let those white boys beat you," they exclaimed. And while there was a dozen people who encouraged me with that same talk, there were just as many who simply gave me the universal sign of black solidarity—the clenched fist held high in the air (popularized by the Black Panther Party during the 1960s and 70s). Although they didn't say any words, the "fist" was their black power salute to let me know we weren't just fighting to advance into the next round of the playoffs. We were fighting for black relevance, and whatever we had to do, we weren't allowed to let "those white boys" beat us.

From the opening tip of the game, they seemed to have the upper hand. We were out-sized. They had two players who stood at least 6 feet, 7 inches, and one who towered above everyone at 6 feet, 10 inches. Now that's tall for even a professional team. So, imagine the nervousness we felt as our tallest player, standing at 6 feet, 6 inches, seemed to get pushed around like a rag doll. I admit I was intimidated. I had yet to play against players with such dominating height. But there was more at stake. We would be fighting for our school's pride. The relevancy of our community and our people. With so much on the line, there was no way we could let these guys get the best of us.

As I mentioned earlier, from the beginning of the game, they seemed to control us. Their rigid, slow-paced style of play was way too much for our fast break showtime-style offense. They were disciplined. They were patient and fundamentally sound. It was as if they were Larry Bird and the 1987 Boston Celtics, and we were the Los Angeles Lakers. Whatever we threw at them, they seemed to have an even better counter attack.

On an early first half play, I was determined to score. Up until that point, we went nearly four minutes without making a basket, and the frustration really began to set in. We were playing against giants, and every shot we launched into the air seemed to be thrown back into our faces. With the courage of David fighting Goliath, I dribbled the ball as fast and as hard as I could. There was only one destination I had in mind, and that was to the basket. So, I attacked. We needed to score. Everything was on the line. The frustration of a potential loss was already beginning to mount, and it was only the first half of the game. We needed a score and I was determined to get it. As I approached the basket, I dribbled around my defender, moving closer to my target. I quickly dribbled to the left, then the right. A quick crossover, then I jumped in the air. I could see the goal. But most importantly, I envisioned the ball going through the basket. I would let nothing stop me. As I jumped to lay the ball in the goal, one of the Katy giants came out of nowhere and caught the ball in the middle of the air.

The only problem was, I had not let go of the ball yet. I was still holding onto the ball, with my feet dangling off the floor. For at least three seconds, my frail body dangled while holding onto the ball of this apparent giant. It was unfair, disrespectful, and completely embarrassing. For him, it was like taking candy from a baby. It was as if I was the kindergartner crying for the neighborhood bully to return my ball. My pride was hurt as laughter filled the arena. Shortly after, we concluded the first half, facing a significant double-digit deficit.

The mood in the locker room at halftime was depressed. Half of our team seemed to already feel this was going to be the last game of our season, while others appeared to hopelessly search for any sign to suggest we had an opportunity to win the game. Our chances for a win looked bleak. But again, as a leader on the team, I was unwilling to bow down and accept defeat so easily. This game wasn't merely just to advance in the playoffs. We were competing for our community. If nothing else, the pride of that responsibility should have been enough to encourage us to go down fighting.

Our coach was not happy. We were the defending state champions and until then, we completely stunk up the gym. He shared a few "interesting" words to let us know just that. And if a good athletic cursing wasn't motivation enough, he went on to state aloud what almost everyone else, including me, in the locker room was thinking:

"Y'all are letting these white boys beat the hell out of you! And you're not doing anything about it," he exclaimed.

I can't speak for anyone else; but that was all the motivation I needed. "We can't let these white boys beat us," I said to Jermaine, one of my younger teammates.

Returning my words with the robotic, stoic stare he was known for, he simply replied with a drab, "Okay."

While his voice answered in the affirmative, the expression in his eyes seemed to wonder if I was participating in the same game he was. "Did you see that guy just catch you in the middle of the air with your legs dangling off the floor?" his eyes seemed to ask.

I didn't care if Jermaine (or anyone else) was with me or not. I was determined to do everything in my power to ensure we would not lose the game. I would not go out without a fight. There was too much at stake.

The second half of the game was a completely different story. We came out of the locker room with the ferocity of the Tasmanian Devil. We defended. We rebounded and scored. I had never seen our team play with such aggressiveness as every shot we threw up, went in. We filled the gym with buckets. With each play, we gradually dug ourselves out of the embarrassing hole we made for ourselves in the first half. Their lead quickly evaporated from double digits down to nine points. Then down to seven. Five. Down three. Finally, we were down by only one point and that was when it happened.

Now the pressure was on them as they scurried around the court in a panic. Just like we couldn't let those white boys beat us, they were also fighting for much more than a continued playoff appearance, as they also couldn't concede defeat to a bunch of black boys. The intensity was high. The crowd of spectators was dangerously charged with the emotions of what was now a dogfight.

At this point, our fast-paced style had the upper hand. A series of their missed shots quickly answered with several quick, fast break points of our own, easily transformed the slow, methodically paced game from the first half into a high-octane shootout. Five minutes passed from the start of the half, and it was quite evident the Katy Tigers were fighting us but they were also fighting the effects of fatigue. To borrow a boxing analogy, we had them on the ropes and it was now time to deliver the knockout punch. In an attempt to slow the game's pace to one they were more comfortable with, one of their guards patiently dribbled the ball up the right side of the court.

On this particular play, we backed all of our defenders to half court, abandoning the full court press we began the second half with (and had become known for). A full court press is a defensive play that intensely puts pressure on the person handling the basketball for the full length of the basketball court. It's often used to speed up the pace of the game and cause the other team to make mistakes and turn the ball over. We often engaged in such pressure tactics against our opponents. Frankly, it was the primary defensive strategy we used during our state championship run. But on this particular play, we backed off.

As their player dribbled across the half court line, we quickly re-applied our defensive pressure, taking him by surprise. The pressure of our defense rattled him so much, he quickly passed the ball as if it were a hand grenade ready to detonate. Without looking, he heaved the ball to the other side of the court, hoping it would magically land in the hands of one of his teammates. Instead, his play of desperation was our saving grace as I capitalized on his mistake and intercepted the ball. The crowd was in an uproar. We now had the ball, making a mad dash to take the lead. I passed the ball to my teammate, Corey, who was running ahead. After two dribbles, Corey then passed the ball back to me. We now only had one defender to beat—a 6-foot, 6-inch defender whose sole purpose was to prevent me from scoring. By now, the defender had positioned himself between me and the basket, eyeing me with the determination to take me out.

Sometimes in life you must develop selective amnesia, and this was one of those times. Previously, in the first half of the game, I was greatly embarrassed by one of their bigger players when I attempted to score in a similar way. However, this time I couldn't let these *white boys* get the best of me. So, I quickly dismissed my previous first half failure, planted both feet on the floor and jumped as high as I could. My 160-pound frame easily surrendered almost eight inches and maybe forty pounds to my opponent. But that didn't matter. My pride, plus the exciting energy from the cheering of the crowd, negated any disadvantage I may have originally experienced. Seeing me jump, he also leapt into the air, intending to block my shot. I rose in the air and so did he. Somehow, I kept rising and rising, as if I were riding an invisible elevator to the top floor of a tall skyscraper. Rising above him, I extended my arm into the rim of the goal and dunked the basketball with a ferocity that rivaled any NBA slam dunk champion.

I conquered the beast. We took the lead. The crowd erupted, and the giants of Katy had been delivered a blow they would never recover from. That play gave our team the courage and momentum needed to win the game. We beat those "white boys." I admit that moment was one of the highlights of my high school basketball career.

Although we had won the state championship the year before, this moment could have easily ranked right there in importance. I would love to be able to say we went on to win our second straight state title that year, but we didn't. The very next week, we lost to Booker T. Washington High School — a predominantly black high school located in the innermost parts of Houston. And although the joy of winning another state title escaped us, there was little sadness. In fact, the day after the loss to Booker T. Washington, we found peace because at least we beat those white boys (of Katy).

Now why do I bring this up? I bring this up to contextually illustrate the paradigm of the black cultural experience in which I grew up, highlighting that the only lens through which I viewed any interaction with white people was the lens of competition. Through the competitive lens, you either dominate or get dominated. There are no in-betweens. Someone is always better. This is the paradigm from which all my interaction with white people was measured. And because there was no way to extrapolate these experiences and thoughts based on the environment, I carried this mentality into other areas of my life — education, business, love, and also, religion. Unfortunately, this is the very mindset that has perpetually restricted the Church from ultimately achieving its purpose, which we will discuss in greater detail later.

THE BIRTH OF BLACK JESUS

P art of me would love to be able to say that my upbringing
was an isolated experience and was not largely indicative
of the overall black cultural experience. But I can't. I can't even
say the competitive paradigm discussed in the previous chapter
is restricted to black folk, as there are too many instances and
examples of its widespread existence in other cultures. So sadly
enough, the struggle of my childhood is an experience that
countless numbers of black people have undergone. It has been
documented for centuries that blacks have fought to establish
minimal levels of significance within the American culture. It's
witnessed in all aspects of society.

And although the Church is supposed to be the one institution where our worldly insecurities and fears are to be overcome by spiritual righteousness, unfortunately, it seems to
take its orders and influence from the worldly systems it was
intended to stamp out. The Church was to be the place where
we were to escape the social and worldly ills haunting and
bounding us. And although blacks tried to obtain various levels
of social significance, at some point in history they came to
realize there would be no reward for their efforts.

For centuries, blacks leaned heavily on their faith to cope
in a society that displayed "no regard for [their] blackness."[2]
It was their spiritual experience that provided the hope and

empowerment needed to "live an authentic human existence in the midst of such disregard."[3] However, through their Christian experience they realized they were unable "to dismantle the sinful structures and attitudes that perpetuated this state of affairs."[4]

Through the black Christian experience, blacks maintained a vibrant hope of a better day. A day of equality. And with equality, there was an expectation of social significance. However, as equality began to manifest in various areas, the social significance did not, thus creating a sense of hopelessness in the midst of their hope-filled religious experiences. Sure, progress had been made for blacks to obtain a seat at the table of mainstream America. However, while sitting at the table, they realized they were sitting on two-legged stools while being served the scraps of yesteryear.

Blacks seeking cultural significance from mainstream America also found they suffered the same levels of insignificance within the Church. As Christianity spread throughout the western world, blacks witnessed few images of their cultural presence within the Church. Illustrations of Bible stories were filled with white characters. Icons of saints and even depictions of Jesus mirrored their European and Caucasian oppressors. So, their insignificance was not only prevalent within mainstream society, but also perpetuated within the very institution where God was to be present. This would especially present a dilemma for black Christians because their faith promoted a hope of an eventual breakdown of the systematic structures that promoted the very social insignificance they wished to overcome. And while their failure to recognize any social equality may have been extremely distracting and discouraging, it wasn't the primary issue black Christians would have to face.

Christianity has always been a religion of hope and faith. Followers of Christ have always been hopeful for a new and better day. So, for black Christians to wait in hope for the day they'd escape cultural degradation would somewhat be within the context of the worldwide Christian experience. Therefore, black Christians would simply need to be encouraged to maintain and continue their faith. Hoping for a better tomorrow while living in the chaos of today describes the history of the Christian experience. This is merely the act of maintaining a present hope for a future promise.

However, delaying the fulfillment of a promise has never negated the promise. It is merely an opportunity to be encouraged and to continue in faith. It's a call to have faith in the One who made the promise and that it will be fulfilled in its perfect time. This is and has been indicative of the Christian experience. Besides, there are several biblical figures who never witnessed the manifestation of their promise; i.e., Abraham and Moses. But that still did not hinder their faith in God.

So again, the realization that blacks did not witness a breakdown of such culturally binding structures is not the crux of the dilemma. However, the presentation of a schizophrenic faith (or religious experience) is. Simply put, what happens when you realize that the same Christian experience (to empower you to overcome such disregard) is the very Christian experience used to support the same disregard you are expecting to overcome? The God in whom I have faith to liberate me is the very God used to subjugate me. This is the dilemma the black Christian faced (and still faces to this day). How is one to solve this?

Interestingly enough, there can only be one of three responses to this dilemma: 1) maintain status quo; 2) totally denounce the current Christian faith and experience; or 3) somehow find a compromise.

On one hand, black Christians could proceed as usual. Continue to promote, support and buy into the very faith consistently used to disregard us culturally, politically, economically and socially. We could continue to worship a god that has continuously encouraged us "to live an authentic human existence in the midst of such disregard," while being the same god used to justify the determination that blacks were only to be considered three-fifths of the human existence they were encouraged and empowered to live.[5] We could very well have continued down that spiritual path to maintain status quo, and many of us have. But to do so comes at a very high cost most have not been willing to pay.

To maintain status quo, black Christians would be required to completely accept the faith pushed down to them by mainstream (white) Christians and disregard the very essence of who many of us think we are, as it would force a self-disregard of our blackness. For most blacks, their blackness is largely all they have to hold onto. Therefore, for most blacks, the response to this dilemma is never anchored in an understanding of spiritual truths, because at no point has it possessed a spiritual root. But it becomes more of an issue of self-preservation. For one to maintain religious status quo, they must trust in a god to liberate them as he continues to disregard them. In layman's terms, it sounds like: *I will let God save me, then beat me and destroy me, only to need more saving.* Hidden behind the disguise of virtue and humility, this ideology works for some blacks. But for most, it's foolishness.

Now the second option to the dilemma at hand is on the complete opposite end of the spectrum. That is, one could totally denounce the current Christian faith and experience altogether. However, for this to be the viable solution, there are two things that must accompany the decision. One, there must be a viable reason to denounce the faith. And second, there must be a viable replacement.

To successfully denounce the faith, black Christians must emotionally, mentally, and spiritually be resigned to the notion that the faith *and* the Christian experience that they have been a part of is fundamentally flawed. In recent years, we have witnessed younger generations of black Christians accept this option more than their older predecessors. That is, because while the first option mentioned earlier comes at a high cost that younger generations don't feel compelled to pay, this option possesses much more risk.

Again, for one to totally denounce their current Christian faith and experience, there must be a viable reason. And that reason must suggest there is a fundamental flaw in the experience and the faith. Now let's go back to the dilemma at hand.

The god I have faith in to liberate me is the very god used to subjugate me. For many, this very reality contradicts the loving nature of God that has been taught. If God loves me so much, then why would He subject me to such an insignificant position? Why would I suffer such degradation? For many, there is no answer to this question that makes any logical sense, and therefore exemplifies a flawed theological construct. And since there's no logical, acceptable answer, the counter-thought becomes, "God must not love me as previously believed *because* I am so insignificant. And if I am insignificant in the real world, I must be insignificant to God." This is very similar to the theological understanding we spoke of in the first chapter. And since it can be argued that all of us are in search of love and significance, once people come to this realization, they will seek a replacement for the faith that was supposed to provide them with godly love and significance. But, there are so many issues with this understanding.

For starters, this approach begs the question: If God loves me, then why would He subject me to and keep me in such an insignificant position? The question itself has a major error and thus can only produce an erroneous response. This question assumes that the subjection of blacks is done *by* the hand of God. No, it's not. Blacks have been subjected by mainstream America. So, by a misunderstanding of whose hand the subjection takes place, we misunderstand the optional actions. Older generations understood this. Therefore, they were still able to maintain their faith in God while understanding that whites were subjecting them in the name of God.

The realization that subjection took place *by* whites *under the name of* God brings one to the understanding that the people are flawed or maybe worse, that certain aspects of the faith that have been passed down may be flawed, but not necessarily the fundamental aspects of the faith. On the other hand, to assume the insignificance is caused *by* God leads people to think everything they've learned about God is false and provides the justification needed to reject the faith entirely. What's worse, this understanding begins to tie the Christian faith experience to whites for whom blacks have already developed a disdain. Thus, it becomes the "White Man's Christianity."

Previously, we stated the first option to the dilemma has a high cost, while the second option has an even greater risk and uncertainty. The first option of maintaining the religious status quo requires a known cost of self-degradation many aren't willing to pay. However, the second option of denouncing the entire faith and Christian experience introduces the *what-if* risk. The *what-if risk* presumes that one's decision to denounce the Christian faith is the correct choice. But, *what-if* it isn't? Are we willing to accept the consequences of an improper decision?

As mentioned before, older generations of black Christians often associated their social degradation with those who actually perpetuated it—white America. Thus, to totally denounce the Christian faith because of works performed at the hands of so-called white Christians would be to denounce the very God they knew and had come to experience spiritually. And to denounce God was to accept a one-way ticket to hell. Therefore, the *what-if* scenario carried too much risk.

On the other hand, more recent generations of black Christians have grown to associate the entire faith (including God) with those who have perpetuated the social degradation of blacks. Therefore, the denunciation of Christianity is not seen as a spiritual detour from God, but rather an objection to *white* Christianity and the *white man's god*. It becomes a denunciation of white people and their faith, as opposed to being directed at God.

But the same *what-if* risk exists here. What if it is a denunciation of God? So, instead of accepting a one-way ticket to hell, there must be a replacement to accompany the reason to denounce the faith. And instead of creating an entirely new faith, many black Christians have offered a compromise — Black Jesus.

Black Jesus is the (for lack of a better word) character based on the notion that Jesus was of African descent and had a darker skin complexion. Black Jesus was born out of black people's need to provide a suitable answer to the everyday dilemma they faced. Black Christians needed to believe in a savior sent to actually save them physically and spiritually. They needed a savior to save them for the purposes of being free, redeemed and significant, as opposed to saving for the purposes of enslaving them all over again. Black Jesus became the black Christians' answer, allowing them to rebel against the establishment while maintaining their Christian righteousness. He (Black Jesus) helps them preserve their blackness, which is of grave importance but also offers enough of a compromise to still walk in their faith. Black Jesus became the answer. Black Jesus provided hope for a better day and cultural significance in the present day. Besides, who wouldn't feel significant knowing the savior of the world looked like them?

Black Jesus was who I came to know as a young boy. In the hallway of our home, we hung a picture of Jesus and his disciples partaking of the Last Supper. All of the disciples were... (you guessed it) black. And in the center of the disciples was a picture of Black Jesus. When I prayed at night, I pictured Black Jesus. He is who my alliance was with.

31

DEAR WHITE JESUS

S o far, we have spoken of the Christian faith and the experience as separate entities. While it's important for us to keep these two important aspects of Christianity separate, I want to ensure there's a mutual understanding of what is meant by the two. There are at least three components of every Christian believer, and each supports and affects the others. You can sort of call it their *Personal Trinity*.

This includes: 1) their personal theological understanding; 2) their physical experiences; and 3) their spiritual encounters (See Fig. 5-1).

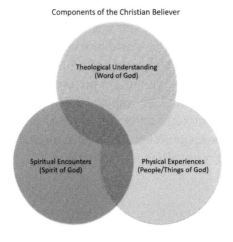

Components of the Christian Believer

Theological Understanding
(Word of God)

Spiritual Encounters
(Spirit of God)

Physical Experiences
(People/Things of God)

Every individual (Christian or not) has come to some kind of theological understanding. That is, their understanding of who God is. Atheists believe God does not exist. For others, it is something different. Regardless of what label they want to be associated with, there is a personal theological understanding of God that has taken place over the course of their lives. For Christians, this theological understanding becomes the foundation of their faith and how they walk out the faith they practice. It is the personal doctrine they adhere to. Therefore, when we refer to the [Christian] faith in this text, we are referring to the believer's fundamental theology of God and Christianity and their application of that theology. It encompasses all the things they have come to know about God—true or untrue. It refers to the doctrine they have come to know and live by. For Christians, this theology is to be based and supported by the Word of God.

Our reference to the Christian experience, on the other hand, actually encompasses the remaining two parts of the Personal Trinity. It entails their spiritual encounters with the Spirit of God and their physical experiences with the people and the things of God. These components combined make up what we are referring to as the experiential portion of Christianity. It refers to the occurrences aiding in the believer's understanding of the faith (religion) they have been exposed to. The spiritual encounter can be anything from dreams, visions, manifestations of the Holy Spirit (speaking in tongues, etc.), to feeling God's presence, or just an overwhelming sense of peace and joy, to name a few. A spiritual encounter may also include what the old saints refer to as "catching the Holy Ghost," or just an old-fashioned nudging from the still small voice in their ear. There's literally no limit to what they may experience during a spiritual encounter with God.

The physical experiences are those emotions and thoughts experienced while interacting with the laypeople, leaders, or things of God. What are their experiences with the people when they attend a worship service? Or, with people who claim to act with God's authority? For example, if they were abused by a spiritual leader from the church, the negative, physical experience could affect how they react to God and godly things. It may result in a personal distrust of church and God. Thus, the overall experience of the believer is defined as the spiritual, physical, emotional, and/or mental happenings experienced by the believer during a religious experience. Each of these components effect the others.

Too much of a reliance on one (or two) components over the others produces a spiritual imbalance in the believer that must be accounted for and dealt with. For example, an over-reliance on doctrine and their personal theology may produce an arrogant and prideful attitude, with them feeling more knowledgeable than others about God. This is a very similar spirit that rested within the Pharisees in the New Testament. An over-reliance on the spiritual encounter may produce Christians who are physically detached from the world in which they live and interact. They become as others may say, "...so *heavenly* minded they're no *earthly* good." And lastly, an intense focus on the physical experience produces unhealthy expectations of the man and/or people of God. This happens when people are distanced from the church because "there are hypocrites in the church." These examples indicate a personal spiritual imbalance within the believer. Not only is this discussion of faith and experience critical to understanding the emergence of Black Jesus, but it is also paramount to understand the next phases of my spiritual journey.

In the previous chapter, *Birth of Black Jesus*, we discussed three options to the dilemma black Christians have faced over the years – the dilemma of worshipping and expecting liberation from a god who is critical in their subjugation. The first of those options was to maintain status quo. The second was to denounce God all together; and third, we saw, was the creation of a compromise—Black Jesus. It's important to note the creation of Black Jesus was due to a reconciliation of black Christians between their personal theological understanding and their Christian experiences. The components of every Christian believer will at some point force a reconciliation between the three. At some point, they will (and must) compare their theological understanding of God with the experiences they have. If those experiences do not align with their theological understanding, there will be a period of reconciliation where the believer may seek experiences to match their theology, or the theology is adjusted to match the experience. The latter is what typically happens in this scenario. Let's look at an example.

The Bible tells us Jesus (and his disciples) healed many. It also refers to God as healer. Now, if in their personal experiences they experienced unanswered prayers during a plea for healing and/or heard of or witnessed false healing reports, their theology may no longer support the belief that God can and will heal them in a time of need. In relation to black Christians, their initial theology spoke of a loving Christ. A loving God. A God who "...so loved the *world*." However, in their experience with white Christians, this love or acceptance wasn't demonstrated. So, their experience with people of God didn't align with what they were taught about God. Instead, they experienced hatred based on how they looked. Therefore, worshipping a Caucasian Jesus would only send reminders of how they were hated by white people. So, the idea of a black Christian experiencing the love of God from a white or European-looking Jesus didn't seem very practical. Thus, Black Jesus became the reconciliation of a personal theology that failed to align with the black Christian's initial experiences. And now this reconciled theology of Black Jesus continues to serve as the backdrop of the present and future black Christian experience. But for me, the Black Jesus theology failed to align with my experiences and I would, therefore, require my own journey.

In August 1995, my older brother and I packed up his tiny, tan 1985 Nissan Sentra and headed north. I was so excited, I completely ignored any frustrations about the grueling, four-teen-hour drive from Houston to Des Moines we had ahead of us. I had just celebrated my high school graduation and now was ready to begin my first year at Drake University.

Space in the car was limited and my brother's large, 6-foot, 7-inch body made our vehicle look more like a clown car than anything that could successfully make the 900-plus mile hike we were embarking upon. It was cramped, and despite the lim-ited space we were working with, I still seemed to pack every-thing I owned. I packed all of my clothes, shoes, books and even toys. I know. I was probably too old to still play with toys. But there were a few action figures I had yet to part with. So, as long as I was going away, they would go away with me.

I can't explain the excitement I felt. I was so excited, I am sure I grinned from ear to ear the entire ride. I even think I grinned in my sleep. He didn't readily admit it, but I think my brother shared a similar excitement. This would be his fifth and final year in college. So, I am sure he was excited to finally see graduation on the horizon. Not to mention, he was also happy to have a family member nearby, as I could imagine it could get pretty lonely being so far away from family.

We packed the car, filling every possible inch of space, and headed north to Iowa—me, my older brother (Marvin) and Ralph. Ralph was my stuffed gorilla toy I received for Christmas in the sixth grade. If Mary had a little lamb, I had a little Ralph. Everywhere I went, Ralph was sure to go. He became sort of a good luck charm for me. As we left, I care-fully positioned Ralph on top of the luggage, ensuring he could "see" the scenery along the way. As we pulled away from the house, my mother appeared to be more nervous than I would have initially expected.

Or maybe nervous wasn't the appropriate word, but rather, prayerful. I had always been the more self-sufficient child. So, my mother rarely worried about my safety or success when going away on trips. Instead of feeling nervous, my mother seemed to pray I wouldn't do anything stupid while away that would get me expelled from school. Given the recent track record I had, I could understand why. I had always been a really good student. But somewhere between seventeen and eighteen years old, I became an unpredictable "Black Power" firecracker. I was becoming more aware of my "blackness," and less aware of politically correct avenues to express the blackness I was ever embracing. Besides, I had recently watched the movie, *Higher Learning*, and was ready to show the world how pro-black I was. *Higher Learning* was a movie that illustrated racial tensions on an American college campus. With my recent zeal for black expression, coupled with the predominantly white environment I would be engulfed in, it was definitely a case for her motherly concern and prayers.

The drive to Iowa wasn't nearly as bad as I had initially expected. Once we exited Texas, the rest of the trip seemed to fly by. I am not sure if you've ever driven on Texas highways, but they are some of the most boring highways I have ever seen. There was no scenery, and it seemed as we were driving the Texas sun was hot on our tail, chasing us out of the state.

Arriving on the campus, I saw (mostly white) people everywhere. Iowa has never been known to have a large black population. According to the United States Census Bureau, only 3.9 percent of Iowa's population was African-American in 2015. This number has increased less than 1 percent between 2010 and 2015.[6] Therefore, the sea of white people before me didn't really come as a shock. Besides, my older brother provided me with a great deal of information on how to handle the culture shock. And while his makeshift class on *How to Deal With White People* would come in handy, I was totally unprepared for the feelings of insecurity that would come during this forewarned culture shock. It was one thing to hear of the lack of diversity, and another to experience it.

When we arrived, my brother pulled the car to the front of a large, four-story brown building and began to unload my belongings.

"This is your dorm," he said. "Goodwin-Kirk. G-K for short. Make sure you don't say the whole name. You don't want to seem like a dork on the first day."

As he unloaded the car, I continued to take in the sights. There were people everywhere. It was a clear summer day. Not a cloud in the sky, with a perfect temperature hovering in the mid-80s. And as the students poured onto campus, I searched for what would seem like a familiar face, a dark face similar to mine, but there was none in sight. Instead, I merely watched as the families unloaded the cars of my new neighbors. And just when I thought there was no chance of my successful survival in this foreign world, I caught a glimpse of another black student. We spotted one another from approximately fifty yards away. As we saw one another, we both gave a refreshing head nod as to say, "I'm here with you brotha," and proceeded to our respective dorm rooms.

After unloading my luggage, I began to settle into my room. By now, my brother left me alone so he could get settled in his off-campus apartment, about two miles away. Typically, freshmen would room with other freshmen. Fortunately, I was able to secure an entire room to myself. So, I had free reign to decorate and arrange the entire room to my liking. That was good, because the previous summer I began my personal "Black Power" movement and decided to decorate my room in all black décor. Everything would be black. The trash can, my luggage and even my clothes hangers were black. Not to mention, the many pictures depicting my blackness I hung on the wall. To make matters worse, while I decorated, I blasted my *black* hip hop music. I wanted everyone to know the black guy was in the building and I wasn't playing any games.

The first week on campus would be a pivotal one for me and would set the tone for much of my adult life. That first week, I went through a *How to Survive in White America* crash course. I wasn't in Houston anymore. Drake University was a complete culture shock, with very few reinforcements. Sure, there were some black students (approximately 120). But to successfully survive, I would need to understand how to navigate the culture I was just thrust into. I would need to know how to communicate and relate. As I met my white counterparts, I practiced my survival skills. I attempted to relate. I attempted to fit in. I even set aside my *black* lingo in an attempt to sound less threatening. But no matter how much I tried to fit in, or how much I tried to relate, I soon came to realize I didn't fit in. I wasn't like *them,* and I couldn't relate.

As I mentioned earlier, in the black community, regardless of what the true story is, you are to look your best at all times. If your family is struggling financially, you're not to look like you're struggling. At all costs, you're to look the part. Dress to impress. This was the case at school, work and at church. Whenever a group of black people are together, you'd better believe they all will be dressed to the hilt, as it often seems like a fashion show. No matter how poor the person, they will look like a millionaire. Well, this was the mentality I took with me to Drake University.

During my first week, I was dressed to impress whenever I went to class or to the student union to eat. Because of this, many white students I ran across made the assumption I came from a privileged background. But my packaging didn't reflect my reality. There's nothing more demoralizing than looking like you are privileged and then running across those who really are. While I worked all summer long to purchase my "Black Power" décor for my dorm room, there were students who truly came from affluent backgrounds. These were the children I read about. The ones I marveled at on television. They were the *Silver Spoons* and *Diff'rent Strokes* kids. They were the children of corporate executives living in posh residences with personal nannies and drivers. They were the children who already travelled the world for family vacations, while my family struggled to make a seven-hour drive to Mississippi for our family reunion. They were the children who flew on private jets, when I had only flown in a commercial airliner once prior, and that ticket was paid for by someone else because my mother couldn't afford to send me on the school-sanctioned trip. These children were familiar with the finest restaurants, while my family was intimidated by Red Lobster because we thought it was too expensive. These children were already assured of management jobs in their parents' corporations, while I was lucky to make it out of my neighborhood. These kids were the part I so desperately sought after. During my first week at Drake, I realized I didn't belong in their crowd. I was out of my league and I hated it. For once, those white boys were beating me, and it began to get the best of me.

One Wednesday afternoon, after a full day of classes and basketball practice, I lay on the bottom bunk in my room, wondering how I could break into the elite crowd. How could I experience the life of the privileged?

"God, I want more for my life. I want to be blessed. I want to experience a life of your favor," I prayed. I wasn't praying for luxury yachts or my own private jet. However, I did desire the finer things in life without the "break-your-back" struggles our family faced over the years. "Jesus, when will we be delivered from the struggle?" I asked aloud.

For years, my family prayed to Jesus for reprieve from our hardships, but to no avail. I was taught God loved us. If so, why would we have to endure such struggle? Where was His blessing? When would it be our turn? I wanted to experience the blessing and favor of God I had been taught about. Where was His blessing on my life?

Unfortunately, in that first week on campus, I realized my turn at the table was nowhere in sight. I simply wasn't good enough and perhaps I never would be. I would never be able to relate and I would never belong to those circles. The blessing I received thus far may be all the blessing I would receive. They (white people) were winning, and quite easily, I might add. I wanted to win. It hurt me that I was close enough for exposure, but too far for experience.

Perhaps it should not have been a competition for me. But sad to say, it was. That's how I was conditioned. It was either black or white. Or better yet, it was always black versus white.

"Jesus, these are the desires of my heart," I prayed.

After weeks of unsuccessful prayers, I had an epiphany. At least, I thought it was an epiphany. It became clear to me there was something white people knew that I didn't. If I was to break into their elite circles and take part in their experiences, I needed to completely immerse myself in their culture. I needed to understand what they understood about family, business, and...religion. That's right. I needed to be baptized into their religion. It was clear my understanding and worship of (Black) Jesus did not yield the results I sought. In fact, what I had been taught of Black Jesus slowly began to lose credibility, as I strongly desired to experience his blessings and redemption.

However, that was not what I experienced. In all my years of worshipping Black Jesus, I merely came face to face with more struggle, heartache and pain. It was time for a change. If I couldn't beat them, I would join them.

During this so-called epiphany, I pledged my allegiance to White Jesus. It would be at that point I would seek to experience the god of the white man, for the sole purpose of winning like the white man. I would put Black Jesus on the bench and substitute him for his paler brother.

"Dear White Jesus," I began. "bless me and give me peace. Grant me with your favor. Amen," I purposefully prayed.

WORSHIPPING UP

As a young boy, I always seemed to have a decent grasp on the importance exposure has on one's life. The more opportunities people have exposure to, the more aware they become of the possibilities and opportunities available to them. The more they are consistently exposed to and required to interact with other cultures, the greater the likelihood they will be accepting of other cultures later in life. Of course, it does depend on whether or not their experiences are primarily positive or negative. But assuming the experiences are positive ones, then this is likely to be the case. The experiences someone is exposed to help shape their reality and outlook on life. Those who have consistent positive exposure to other cultures and opportunities are less inclined to be limited by the social and cultural boundaries society tries to impose on them. Unfortunately, I didn't have consistent exposure to other cultures or many opportunities to see myself past the social limitations.

Because I wasn't exposed to other cultures and opportunities early in my life, I often found myself trying to manufacture opportunities to make up for it. For example, I would take personal field trips to museums and libraries to learn more about other places and cultures. I would even take long drives alone to the more affluent parts of town to gain a sense of the people living there. What were they like? What did they do? How could I be like them? Every home I passed by seemed to beam with happiness, joy, and a level of blessing I had yet to experience. Because I had no true knowledge of the people I observed, I merely created a mental image of what I thought they were like. Whether that image was true or not, it didn't matter. What I saw of their lifestyle was vastly different from my lifestyle. Therefore, my image of them was opposite of the image I had of myself.

Initially, these long drives were intended to encourage me to strive for a better life for myself and my family. It was like a real life vision board. If I could see it, I could achieve it. But sometimes these field trips had an adverse effect. After spending hours in the museum or driving through affluent neighborhoods, I was always required to make the long drive home, which never failed to remind me of how far away I was from being a part of the world I recently visited. It never ceased to remind me that no matter how many times I visited, I still had to go back to my reality—a reality of struggle and hardship. It was a reality where dreams often died or had very little chance to manifest. This reality aided in my pursuit of White Jesus.

Let's be honest here. My (as well as others') pursuit of White Jesus was primarily based on my desire to find significance and be accepted by mainstream white America, all in the name of Jesus Christ. Until I was willing to admit that truth, I would do all I could to experience an increase in social standing by pursuing the Jesus of those who were higher up the social ladder than me.

For most of my school days, I was a part of what's known as the "in crowd." I was popular and there was a level of significance that came with popularity. Regardless of how big (or small) my black world was; I felt significant in it. There was a piece of me that felt like I owned it. But as I transitioned to my adult years, life forced me to adopt a new paradigm. No longer would I be able to operate with the assumption the black community was the epicenter of all life. No longer could I expect the rest of the world around me to understand or appreciate my struggles. There were new ways of thinking. New ways of talking. New ways of dealing with problems. In my early years, everything seemed to be a struggle or a fight. So, when adversity arose, I physically fought those I blamed for my personal struggles. But those rules didn't apply in my new world.

In my early years, I was someone special. I was famous in my neighborhood— "hood famous." I was a star athlete and respected in my community. But, in the *real* world, no one knew my name. No one looked my way and no one cared. When this reality collided with my previous reality, an emptiness emerged. Feelings of worthlessness. Feelings of insignificance. I was no longer in the mainstream and it was causing a huge problem with me internally. I yearned for the privilege and the significance I experienced before. But the environment was no longer the same. I was no longer at the height of my athletic career. I was no longer within the confines of the small black community that had insolated me throughout my childhood. But what was worse, I couldn't go back.

Regardless of how badly I yearned for the significance my previous environment provided me, to go back would mean I would re-enter the very struggle I so desperately wanted to escape. It meant letting my dreams die, or at least putting them on hold for a significant amount of time. And besides, by now I realized there was more out there than what I had grown up seeing. I began to see first-hand the rest of the world was not all about the struggle. Although most of me wanted it, I didn't feel like I belonged in this new world. So, there I was; stuck in the social and personal doldrums of life. I couldn't go backward and didn't quite know how to move forward.

This battle raged within me for many years, as I saw myself trying to toggle between the two social worlds and still maintain my sanity. On one hand, I had my black heritage and the struggle of not "forgetting where I had come from." And on the other hand, I had the desire to be accepted by my mainstream white counterparts, who seemed to represent everything great and exciting about life. In modern American culture, there were always certain things categorized as being "white," referring to things typically experienced by white people. Other things were said to be "black," or things black people would typically do.

For example, scuba diving off the coast of a beautiful island would be considered a *white* person's vacation. On the other hand, spending a day on the dirty beaches of Galveston, Texas, was my *black* vacation. Investing in stocks and other investment vehicles might be a *white* trait, while simply having a checking account and maintaining a negative balance was my *black* experience. Starting your adult life with good credit and significant financial resources was thought to be the *white* experience. On the other hand, having bad credit at twelve years old because one of your relatives used your personal information to get credit was my *black* experience. Therefore, I wanted to switch up my experiences. I wanted to experience what seemed to be privilege and favor, like the white people. So, I began to go where they went. I would do what they did; and I would worship where they would worship.

I understand writing this clearly places me in the line of fire from many in the black culture who would suggest and voice their frustration with my "desire" to be white. But it really wasn't an attempt to be white. Rather, it was a desire for social and cultural significance. We all go through the same quest at some point in our lives. Some people go on this journey, and instead of conforming; they rebel against the very thing they desire, creating their own society or subculture. It's the old *beat 'em* approach. There's a realization they will never be on the inside or in the mainstream, so they create their own version of the mainstream society, aligning with their reality and in some ways mirroring the culture they found themselves excluded from. This is why people place so much significance on their various subcultures. The hip-hop subculture is a prime example of this very point.

But this wasn't the case for me. I found myself on the outside looking into a culture I desperately wanted to be a part of. For most of my life, I lived in an environment where the *beat 'em* approach was the norm. It didn't work for me, as it surely didn't appear to be working for other black people, either. My reality was that I wanted to be in the mainstream. I knew I couldn't beat 'em. Therefore, I enthusiastically sought to *join 'em* (white American culture).

When I moved to Dallas in 2000, one of the first things I wanted to do was to find a good church home. Ironically, the church referrals I received were based on how people perceived me from a socio-economic standpoint.

"Excuse me, I am new to the city. Do you know of a good church I can go to?" I would ask.

"Sure. You're in your early twenties, a nice professional black man. You should visit _____ church," they would often say.

On several occasions, the church recommendations were based on the fact I was a young, black professional, and the particular church would be good for networking purposes or because the recommended church was known to have many attractive single women. Like most, these people merely perpetuated the thought that people of similar cultural, social and economic backgrounds should worship together. Without any consideration for teaching, spiritual experience, etc., they referred me to a church based on what they thought would make me comfortable. Unbeknownst to them, I wasn't looking to be grouped with people like me. I desired something different.

Besides, by this time, the black church had failed to provide me with the significance I was searching for. Even sermons telling me Jesus looked like me seemed to miss the mark in giving me what I needed. The Jesus I worshipped growing up was associated with a struggling people. He was the Jesus of our struggling household. He was the Jesus of depression and stress. Additionally, as a young man, I couldn't get behind a Jesus who represented so much struggle. I wanted the other guy. I wanted the Jesus who "blessed" His people. I wanted the Jesus who made his people the head and not the tail (Deut. 28:13). For as much as I could see, my people were always the tail, and it didn't look like it was going to change any time soon.

So, I attended as many white churches as I could find in search of White Jesus. I attended Methodist, Episcopalian, Baptist and non-denominational churches. Believe it or not, I even went to a Greek Orthodox church, searching for White Jesus. Now, that was an interesting experience. I attended predominantly white churches in Iowa, Georgia and Texas. But, no matter what church I attended, I still felt empty. I still felt like I didn't belong. In every church I went to, I experienced people looking at me like I truly didn't belong. It was as if they all thought I was lost.

Recently when walking through the shopping mall, I ran into Scott, a white friend of mine I hadn't seen in at least eighteen months. Scott and I worked together a few years prior, and had always seemed to have a good relationship. Many people discourage you from talking about your faith at work. But Scott and I seldom followed that advice. He always had questions about the Bible and his faith. For him, having answers to his religious inquiries was important, especially since he was starting a new family at the time. So, each day Scott would come to work with questions on his mind, eager to learn and hear my responses. So, it was a pleasant surprise to see Scott and for us to catch up with one another.

After exchanging pleasantries, Scott seemed to resume where we had left off months ago, by asking me questions about ministry and theology. I was aware he and his family hadn't been consistently attending a church. So, I invited Scott and his family to visit our church and worship with us. Scott never hid what he was thinking, and our relationship grew to where he realized I wasn't easily offended. So, although his next question took me by surprise, it didn't surprise me he'd have the nerve to ask it.

After I presented my invitation for him and his family to worship with us, he asked, "Do you guys allow people like me at your church?"

Scott wanted to know if we *allowed* white people in our worship services. Whether we allowed it or not, he wanted to feel comfortable and free to worship without feeling alienated. The interesting part of this question was that it was based on Scott's experiences. And looking back at some of my previous experiences with worshipping in predominantly white churches, I can understand why Scott felt the need to ask. Most of the predominantly white churches I went to made me feel the same way—alienated and as if I wasn't wanted there.

After I assured Scott he and his family would feel welcomed at our worship services, he agreed to think about visiting. To this day, Scott has not taken advantage of my invitation. I am sure the weight of his previous experiences and concerns was more than the assurances I could possibly give him. I understood Scott's point of view. Besides, I often felt alienated when worshipping with predominantly white congregations. However, I was willing to undergo such alienation to obtain an affiliation with the privileged. Unfortunately, Scott would have had to pay a different price.

There is a phrase society uses: "marrying up." This is where someone from a lower socio-economic status marries someone in a higher class for the sake of obtaining social, cultural and financial significance. This was me. Instead, I was using the church as my desired springboard to propel me to the higher social classes. I was like a young poor girl looking for a wealthy husband to rescue her out of the ghetto. While she would be on her quest to move up the social and economic ranks by marrying up, I was looking to do the same thing by worshipping up.

Despite what many may think, my pursuit to worship up didn't simply begin by waking up one day with a desire to worship with white people. In fact, it began long before I ever stepped foot in a predominantly white church. If you hadn't guessed, I wasn't a fan of the continuous struggle I experienced growing up. During my childhood, I made every effort to get out of that environment. I studied and I worked hard until I finally escaped. But I wasn't so much concerned with escaping a particular location or geography, as I was a particular mindset.

For many Christians, both black and white, there's honor in the struggle. But I always thought there was even more honor in overcoming the struggle. Besides, Paul states in Romans 8:37, "we are more than conquerors through Him that loved us." Unfortunately, the black church seemed to get its strength from the struggle. It unified and appeared to empower us. At some point, I wanted to get past the struggle. An inability to forget the struggle is often a cry less fortunate blacks hurl at more accomplished members of their same culture. "You've forgotten where you've come from," many will say, attempting to challenge one's loyalty to the struggle, or the 'hood. The struggle is the foundation of black secular and Christian culture. But, as long as the black church continues to rely on the struggle as the foundation of its work and unity, it will continue to perpetuate what it seems to fight. As long as we continue to focus on the struggle, we will continue to get the struggle.

In his book, *When God Was Black,* Bob Harrison writes to the black church:

> In this light we must stop feeling sorry for our black skin which brings injustice and discrimination. Isn't God bigger than these? If He can feed a multitude, heal the sick, raise the dead, overcome the devil himself, do you think for a moment that He can't overcome any apparent disadvantages of our blackness and all it represents?[7]

When I first began to pastor, I received a word of caution from one of my associates. "Don't expect to have a truly diverse ministry like some of the others you see. Blacks don't have a problem sitting under a white pastor because to them, it's like a status upgrade. But very few whites can take spiritual guidance from a black pastor. They can't go backward," he said. Since I heard those words, I have been determined to find a case to prove him wrong. Sure, there are some churches out there where this isn't the case; but they have been few and far between.

Church congregations always reflect the characteristics of its pastoral leadership. Most pastors and leadership preach and teach from their own experiences. This should be based on their spiritual experiences, but it is often only from their physical life experiences. For black church leaders, those physical life experiences are centered around the struggle of being black. As a leader, I cannot lead the congregation to a place I have not been. For many black pastors, the struggle is still very relevant to them. They grew up in the struggle. Like me, their environments often perpetuated the struggle. And as a black community leader, there's pressure to still participate and be actively engaged in the struggle. So unfortunately, many of them have not been able to put the struggle behind them and overcome it. Therefore, they are unable to teach and help their congregations to overcome it without making it a foundational reality for them.

On the other hand, white congregants aren't familiar with the (black) struggle, because of what's called "white privilege." This refers to the everyday social privileges white people are said to experience because they are white—regardless of where they may be on the social or economic totem pole. If they are white, they are thought to be the recipient of some sort of privilege because of it. It is often believed the lowest white person (socially) starts with a greater advantage than most black people. So, they often can't relate to the constant inference of the struggle witnessed throughout many black congregations. For the black pastor to lead the white congregant in spiritual growth, he must do so apart from the struggle, which cannot be done unless he or she has overcome it.

Secondly, racial socioeconomic inequality is often viewed differently between minorities and whites. While blacks and Hispanics often cite discrimination for its cause, whites view it as an issue of personal motivation (or lack thereof).[8] Research suggests ideas of racial inequality become similar across multicultural congregations and often take the view of the majority (or of its leader).[9] This means for whites to consistently worship under the leadership of a black pastor or be a part of a predominantly black congregation, there would be a greater chance their view of racial inequality would conform to their black counterparts. This is often a cost whites are not willing to pay. However, it is a cost many minorities are willing to pay, especially if they are already more inclined to adopt the white voice anyway.[10] Hence, minorities are more willing to "worship up" than whites are willing to "worship down."

Despite the words of caution I initially received from my fellow pastor, I believe the Church is ripe for a move of God which will shatter the color line. At that time, there will be no more distinctions between the white church and black church. No more will there be such a thing as worshipping up or down, but it will just be pure worship. For clarity, let me state I am not referring to a church where whites can simply feel welcomed to worship with blacks or vice versa, because that would simply be an integrated white or black church. I am not referring to mere integration between believers. I am referring to a Church where you can't tell the difference. A church where there is no majority; there are only believers in Christ. One Body. In the words of Bob Harrison, "May Christians of all colors join together to bring victory. For the enemy is not the white man or the black man but the devil himself. Let us together be more than conquerors for Christ."[11]

THE TWILIGHT ZONE OF WORSHIP

As a child, I asked my mother why we didn't worship with white people. To this day, I still do not know what made me ask that question. But after giving me a confused look as if to question why I would even desire such a thing, she proceeded to explain to me about the differences in our worship styles. Her emphasis centered on the different styles in music.

"We like more upbeat music. While their music is a little more…" She paused. I could tell she struggled to find a politically correct description for what she wanted to convey. If you knew my mother, politeness was not one of her strongest qualities. So, to find the appropriate word was a tremendous struggle for her. But after what seemed to be an eternity of her trying to find a polite word to describe her understanding of the white worship service, she gave up, blurting out, "…boring. Yeah, their services are more boring."

Although at that time I hadn't yet attended a worship service with our white brothers and sisters, I knew one thing. The black church was not boring. In fact, it was often the most entertainment I would often experience throughout the week. As a young boy, the one thing I had to look forward to when I went to church was to be entertained. So, while I respected her candor, part of me wondered exactly how much of what she told me was based on personal experience versus hearsay. In my adult years, I would discover exactly what my mother referred to when she described the worship differences between whites and blacks. In fact, these differences would be a major source of contention in my spiritual life and worship experience.

I spent years of my young adult life searching after the white worship experience. Granted, the primary reason for my feverish pursuit was to adopt a greater sense of self-worth and to have White Jesus deliver me from the realization of the constant struggle often perpetuated through the black worship experience. However, during my pursuit, and once I successfully assimilated into the white worship experience, the feelings I thought I would eventually obtain escaped me for several reasons.

The first reason my pursuit often ended in futility is because for most of it, I found myself walking into a white church where the doors were opened to me, but the worship experience was still not. As stated in the book, *Black Fire Reader*, "Every black Christian in America has had dozens of experiences where he has been offered something but only in politeness. He must not only hear that he is welcome, but he must see demonstrated that he is definitely wanted."[12] This statement speaks greatly to me as I remember how I sought to experience White Jesus. In no way did anyone physically turn me away. However, the love we have been charged to display was often not the center of these experiences. And white believers drawn to the black Christian experience reflected the same sentiments. So, when Scott (mentioned in the previous chapter) asked if our church *accepts people like him*, he wasn't asking if our doors were opened to him. What he was concerned with was whether or not he and his family would be genuinely wanted.

The second reason my attempt to worship on the *other side* didn't provide me with the feelings I desired *was* because of the differences between the worship services, but not in the way my mother previously described. Overall, I didn't find the white

Christian experience to be *that* boring. Except for the time I went to the Greek Orthodox Church. Now that was boring. But regarding the white worship experience, I am not saying it was as entertaining as the black church, but I definitely wouldn't suggest the overall experience to be disregarded because it is boring. Boring? No. Different? Yes. And it *was* this difference that would bring about a conflict, preventing me from feeling at home in either the black or the white church. It was as if I was trapped in a twilight zone of worship experiences with no way to get out.

As I stated earlier, the black church always provided me with my much-needed dose of entertainment for the week. As a kid (and even as an adult and a pastor), I always found something entertaining taking place within the black church. The preacher was sure to be animated while the random acts of the Spirit would provide comic relief to all children present. But what most people, including my mother, often took notice of was the upbeat style of the music. The black Christian worship experience is all about the music. There's music in basically every part of the worship service. The sermon itself is often sung in a rhythmic pattern, often referred to as *whooping*. So, in the black church, "the service is really drama with music. And since music without motion is unnatural among Negroes, there is always something that approaches dancing—in fact *IS* dancing—in such a ceremony."[13] And as the music continues to lead the congregants to a particular level of enchantment, one may easily hear the rings of great shouts fill the air in the black church. These shouts are often an indication the shouter has encountered God in a particular way, so powerful and overwhelming it causes one to release an uncontrollable shout.

Many aspects of the black church experience stem from the spiritual roots of its African predecessors. Even shouting was "nothing more than an African possession by the gods. The gods possess the body of the worshipper and he or she is supposed to know nothing of their actions until the god decamps."[14] For blacks, this is a style of worship inherent in our DNA. It's a part of our culture and cannot, nor will it be forfeited. To forfeit this aspect of the worship experience is to engage in self-denial. But for whites, many of the traditions of the black worship experience have historically been categorized as antics of the uneducated. The dancing, shouting and whooping by its preachers have all been used to broadly paint the black church with a label as an uneducated church. To blacks, it represents a Spirit-filled experience. To others, it's considered entertainment.

Ironically, whites have not completely discarded all aspects of the black worship experience. One of the largest and fastest growing Christian denominations in America has been the Church of God in Christ (COGIC), a denomination founded on the black slave religious experience.[15] However, its growth has not gone unnoticed by many mainstream white denominations and churches. Seeking to grow their own churches and appeal to a more modern generation of believers, many white churches have sought to inject their services with the entertaining drama and music derived from the black church, attempting to revitalize services often thought to be dead and boring. White churches across America began to include black gospel songs in their worship lineups to draw in a more diverse crowd, and to add a sense of entertainment to services previously void of any emotion or excitement.

Furthermore, many churches sought to add as much entertainment to their services as possible, including entertaining sermons, including props and various theatrics. I heard some pastors refer to this as "inner-tainment" instead of entertainment, suggesting the form of entertainment displayed within the church is beneficial for one's internal soul. This focus on making church services more entertaining is the basis of the seeker-sensitive church movement, which has led to the rise of many mega-ministries. These churches operate on the belief that if you keep people entertained during church, they will be more willing to attend the services. The more entertaining the service, the more people will come and stay. This recent injection of entertainment within the white church reminds me of a statement someone told me early in my ministry. They said, "People don't want to change. They merely want to be entertained while talking about it [change]." The churches within the new seeker-sensitive movement appeared to embrace this very sentiment. Hence, the push for entertaining services and programs.

While the black church has been perceived to be entertaining from the beginning, the white church seems to be relying on its own form of entertainment as well. Unfortunately, the passion that drove the black church for centuries and has been the source of its entertaining worship experience cannot be imitated. So, during my transition to the white Christian experience, I missed the passion rooted in the black church. As entertaining as the lights and worship bands were, I still yearned for the passion of Black Jesus.

While aspects of the black Christian experience were valuable enough to borrow and infuse into the white church, black Christians had a very difficult time shaking the stigma of being uneducated. Dating back to the early 1900s, this categorization was initially placed on all Pentecostal Christians—black and white—by more traditional Evangelicals. A primary characteristic of Pentecostalism is the belief in baptism by the Holy Spirit, evidenced by speaking in tongues. Speaking in tongues is a primary belief of white and black Pentecostals alike. However, many traditional Christians saw the actions of Pentecostals as being out of control, wild and disruptive. But as racial divides were erected within the Pentecostal denominations, blacks saw it virtually impossible to shake the uneducated stigma, while this was not necessarily the case with their white Pentecostal counterparts. This is largely because of the isolated nature of the worship experience, coupled with the discriminatory practices of the American society at the time, and the adopted African religious traditions which continue to be visible within the black church.

The worship experience has been and continues to be quite isolated. That is, they take place on specific days among a specific group of people. The majority of the people attending the worship services did so with similar expectations. Simply put, Pentecostals often worshipped with Pentecostals. So, the Pentecostal worship experience that included speaking in tongues was a normal and expected occurrence among Pentecostals, whether they were white or black. However, outside of the worship services in daily life, white Pentecostals were still white while black Pentecostals were still black. White Pentecostals would have been looked upon as uneducated because of the demonstration of their spiritual experiences, while blacks were thought to be uneducated by nature. At their core, they (blacks) were seen as uneducated. Therefore, white Pentecostals would receive what I would call, a 'white pass,' while blacks struggled to expel their uneducated label. Well into the late 20th century, black Christian leaders sought to deny this stigma placed on the black Christian.

Black Christians were also considered uneducated because of the various African religious traditions that remained within the black Church. One in particular is the tradition of whooping by the black preacher. In an article discussing whooping within the black church, John Blake defines whooping as "a celebratory style of black preaching that pastors typically use to close a sermon. Some church scholars compare it to the opera; it's that moment the sermon segues into song. Whooping pastors use chanting, melody and call-and-response preaching to reach parishioners in a place where abstract preaching cannot penetrate."[16] If the scripture is considered to be the meal, the whoop would be the special sauce making the meal worth eating. Whooping roots can be traced back to the musical focus of the African religious experience and continues to link the black Christian to its religious past. Whooping has been such a staple within the black church, it is said many black seminary students across the country can be found practicing their whoop for future congregations. It's the continuation of such African religious traditions helping fuel the stigma of the uneducated black Christian.

Many whooping preachers have recently undergone strict criticism from those black church leaders seeking to erase the previous stigmas. For years, many black preachers have depended so much on the whoop, they have been accused of neglecting to provide any substance to the messages they deliver to the congregations. In fact, I have experienced this on many occasions.

One Sunday, I visited an old Baptist church in Vicksburg, Mississippi. Now if you've never gone to a country church, there's none like a country Mississippi church, where you are bound to get some good old-fashioned whooping. On this particular Sunday, there was a guest preacher, Reverend King (no relation; at least I don't think we were related). Reverend King was a small old man. You could tell he had been preaching for a long time. I must admit, I was pretty excited to see Reverend King approach the pulpit to deliver his message. The church on this particular Sunday was extremely hot because the air conditioner had gone out. To limit the sweat pouring down our faces, many people fanned themselves with handheld paper fans adorned with a portrait of Martin Luther King, Jr. Everything about this church service was a cliché of the black church experience. The people were dressed in their finest threads. And the service was long and hot. So, when Reverend King finally approached the pulpit, I was quite excited. As the small man began, I expected opening remarks, a story, or even a contextual scripture or two. But that's not what happened. Without any warning or lead in by the organist, Reverend King began whooping. And he whooped for more than an hour. I don't know if he ever read a scripture or had a message other than his whoop.

Unfortunately, I have had experiences where the preacher's message is all whoop and little to no substance far too many times. It is this phenomenon of the whoop that aided in the difficulty for many black Christians to expel the stigma of being uneducated. It is also the phenomenon of the whoop that provided me with a large feeling of displacement within the black church. Although I could easily relate to the black worship experience, my unfulfilled desire for spiritual nourishment led me to seek satisfaction elsewhere. I am not saying *all* whooping preachers lack substance in their messages. However, I believe far too many have focused on the whoop, or the gravy, and have not given necessary attention to the actual meat.

While the black church provided me with a passionate and an entertaining worship experience, I felt there were things lacking in my ability to understand spiritual things. However, on the other hand, whooping was not something you would typically experience at a white church. White preachers' sermons would be delivered in a style more congruent to a lecture in a college auditorium. It would possess a primary scripture and contain at least three points. Compared to the typical black whooping preacher, the style of the white preacher would be considered boring. Besides, for black preachers, many congregants don't express their satisfaction with the sermon until he starts whooping. After a good session of whooping, you can often hear members of the congregation saying, "Man, he sure did preach." But if asked what the message was about or what was learned from the message, you will often receive a blank stare, because many aren't able to recall any lessons learned.

To the black Christian, preaching is not preaching without whooping. So, for the black Christian who is accustomed to the activities of the black whooping preacher, the white preacher is not a preacher, but merely a lecturer.[17] So while the black Christian thought the white experience lacked power and passion, the white Christian thought the black to be uneducated and merely an entertainer. And since the religious leaders represented what was perceived to be the best of our culture, the others were deemed uneducated as well.

I mentioned earlier that although there was a serious lack of respect for the black Christian experience, whites sought to swipe aspects of the black worship experience and infuse them into their own. The same was the case with the black church. To combat the stigma of being uneducated, many black church leaders began to abandon the whoop from their messages and go to a teaching style of delivery in an attempt to appeal to a more educated audience. The abandonment of whooping has also been criticized within black Christian circles, described as a result of "self-hate" and disdain for the black culture by black Christian leaders, who may feel they have arrived socially and economically.[18] In a discussion of the black Christian response to blacks who adopt the white Christian experience, Estrelda Alexander states:

> *The real singing Negro derides the Negro who adopts the white man's ways in the same manner. They say of that type of preacher, "Why he don't preach at all. He just lectures."*

> *And the way they say the word "lecture" make[s] it sound like horse-stealing. "Why, he sound like a white man preaching." There is great respect for the white man as lawgiver, banker, builder, and the like but the folk Negro do not crave his religion at all. They are not angry about it; they merely pity him because it is generally held that he just can't do any better that way. But the Negro who imitates the whites comes in for spitting scorn.[19]*

Herein lies the foundation of my dilemma. While the passion of the black worship experience was definitely something

I could relate to, there was a strong yearning for the educational appeal of the white message. My desire for one was innate. It's what I had known all of my life. However, my desire for the other was acquired and could distance me from my roots. On one side of the fence, I was entertained, but had many spiritual and biblical questions left unanswered. On the other side of the fence, I would become more knowledgeable while lacking the passionate connection I needed during worship. What ensued was a consistent game of worship hokey-pokey. I would dip my right foot on one side; take it out. Then dip my right foot on the other side and shake it all about. (I really didn't shake my foot. But hopefully, you get the picture.) At some point, I would be forced to make a decision. When the time came, I simply decided to withdraw from the Church. Sure, I would attend a church service on special occasions or when I was invited by friends. But there was no connection to the Church or its mission at the time. I simply took residence in the twilight zone of worship and wouldn't find my way out for some time.

BLACK JESUS, WHITE JESUS

I sat attentively on the end of a pew toward the back of the church. At the time, this seat seemed appropriate. It was close to the exit, giving me an advantage to escape the mad dash of people sure to rush out of the building once the service was over. It was the perfect spot for me to remain anonymous. It was close enough to the action for me to feel present, but far enough away for me to not draw any unwanted attention to myself. I was new to the city and new to this church. God forbid if this was one of those churches requiring new visitors to stand up and be acknowledged by the entire congregation. Although I knew very few people in the area, I was not at all interested in having a swarm of people overwhelm me and remind me that I was the outsider by welcoming me to their church. Maybe I would have been more welcoming to the idea had this been a smaller congregation. But there were so many people. Hundreds. So, the idea of being showered with "new guy" affection from so many people wasn't one of the experiences I looked forward to. So, sitting toward the back of the church allowed me to find comfort in my social awkwardness and maintain a more desired sense of invisibility.

Several weeks prior, my job relocated me to Dallas from Atlanta. Although I was still focused on my pursuit of White Jesus, the black church at this time provided me with a level of security as I prepared to begin this new chapter of my professional and social life. By now, several years had passed since I became intrigued with pursuing White Jesus, and even more time had passed since I left my childhood home. I graduated from college and was working in corporate America. So, much of my new life—my work, my neighborhood and many of my social activities, had very much become integrated. My life was changing. My professional and economic status had changed. No longer was I the young, black kid from an impoverished home. Now, I was a computer systems engineer at a Fortune 100 company. My social status was changing and so did my address. No longer was I expected to live in the dilapidated areas among the city's forgotten. I could now "move up" and dwell among the middle class.

So, when moving to Dallas, I quickly darted to the northern suburbs of the city, to easily illustrate my newfound social status amongst the 'haves,' leaving behind any resemblance of my affiliation with the other side of the tracks. At the time, Dallas seemed to possess an invisible line of social demarcation between the "haves" and the "have-nots" of the city. Like several American cities, Dallas's freeway system seemed to separate the privileged from the less fortunate. It's a line separating areas of great investment and growth from those areas city officials planned to let deteriorate. So, just like my religious preference of being on the winning religious team, I also wanted to be on the winning side of the social and economic scene. I wanted to be where the affluent and privileged were. I wanted to be on the side of the "haves." But every Sunday, I was perfectly comfortable getting dressed in my finest clothes and driving thirty or more minutes, crossing the "tracks" to worship with my southern "brothas and sistahs" in the black church. Not only would the black church provide me with a level of familiarity in this foreign land, but it would also give me that weekly injection I needed to stay in touch with my people. It would be my weekend mistress, keeping me in contact with Black Jesus as I

63

pursued a love interest with White Jesus during the week. So, as I took my place toward the back of the church, I intentionally absorbed every aspect of the worship service serving as a connection to my people.

The worship music was upbeat. Energetic. It was the kind of music that regardless of whether or not you truly liked the song, the beat alone would force at least a foot tap. The congregation clapped together. They shouted and sang along. They were all unified, singing. Some danced in connection with the music in their seats. The music was infectious and seemed to also overtake me as I made every attempt to keep my cool and remain still. The louder the choir sang, the more energized the crowd became. After a few minutes of taking it all in, I joined them. Clapping, singing and dancing to the beat in my seat. This was the black church experience in all its finest. And because I was consumed by my pursuit of White Jesus in recent years, it was what I longed for—to have my body energized and taken over by some good old-fashioned gospel singing.

After the singing and the offering period (this is when everyone gives tithes and monetary offerings to the church) were completed, the pastor approached the podium to prepare to give his message. As he approached, the congregation welcomed him with a raving applause, almost like what you would experience at a rock concert. It was quite evident he was well-liked among the people and gained some notoriety within Christian circles. But this was not anything new to me. Pastors in the black church, especially those who achieved some level of notoriety, are often treated as rock stars. Their congregations often hold them in the highest regard, and this pastor was no different. Over the years, he had been influential within the community and in black Christian circles, thereby earning him applause double that of any "normal" preacher. I heard a lot of great things about this pastor in particular and must admit, I was pretty excited and interested in what he had to say.

When he began speaking, it was quite evident he was very charismatic and equally eloquent. His use of the English language was magnificent. The alliterations and illustrations seemed to be masterfully placed at specific moments within the sermon to draw distinct reactions and applause from the audience. He was an orator. A griot of magnificent proportion. In African culture, a griot was one who possessed the responsibility of maintaining the oral history of the tribe. They often did this through poems and stories. This pastor was not only knowledgeable, but a master spokesman. "If I were to have the opportunity to speak to large audiences, I want the ability to speak like him," I thought.

However, as I continued listening, I realized I was more enamored with his creative prose than his actual message. No disrespect intended. While very eloquent, the message seemed very familiar. Not that I thought he copied it from someone else. Rather, the point of the message was one I was familiar with, as it was intended to ignite a spark within the black community. It appeared to be focused less on promoting the spiritual depth of its listeners and more of a rally cry for black people. After about fifteen minutes into the message, I felt like I was at a Black Power rally. Interestingly enough, I wasn't surprised. Besides, it was February.

As many are aware, February is observed as Black History month in the U.S. This is when most of the country (primarily African-Americans) recognize and celebrate the accomplishments of black people throughout its history. Given the black church has been and continues to be the cornerstone of African-American culture, it's only expected they would also contribute to and maintain the recognition of its people, both in American history and biblical history. And in his message, this pastor ensured he did his part to inject black pride into what he considered an apathetic generation of black folk. Referring to the story of the Ethiopian eunuch (Acts 8:26-40), he carefully used the scripture and his knowledge of Bible history to highlight that black people were not absent from the history of the Church.

"It was an Ethiopian, a black man, that helped spread the gospel to Africa," he said. "Ethiopians. These are Africans— black people. And they all held significant positions in biblical history. Simon of Cyrene, a black man, helped carry the cross of Jesus," he reported, referring to Mark 15:21.

Example after example, he used to convey his message that black people are not insignificant and played a major role in the faith we have been largely absent from. With each example, the congregation got rowdier and rowdier to encourage him to continue. It was a rally. It was a wake-up call. But more so, it was an emotional plea to the black congregants to accept our rightful place of significance because our history was one of significance. Just when I thought he received his necessary approval from the congregation (which is when most preachers begin to bring their message to a close), he gathered what we call in sports "his second wind," and announced with even more fervor, "and if I see one more picture of a white frail-looking Jesus, I am going to scream. Jesus was black," he yelled, as the audience greeted his words with uproarious praise.

Now, the debate about Jesus' ethnicity has been an ongoing one for quite some time. I wouldn't even say it's a theological debate, because to my understanding, there are no theological grounds to confirm or deny this claim. The debate of Jesus' skin color is more of an anthropological discussion, where some often try to include biblical text as some sort of reference. Theologically, we can and will argue the debate of Jesus' skin color has absolutely no positive effect on the kingdom of God and the role the Church plays in His kingdom. However, sociologically, it has proven to be of great importance, which we will discuss later. Nevertheless, the idea and image of Black Jesus seemed to rally black Christians like never before. So, the pastor's public decree of his allegiance to Black Jesus sent the congregation in an uproar.

I must admit, it made me a little uncomfortable. Not because I had been straddling the fence between White Jesus and Black Jesus for the past several years; but because something in my spirit just couldn't seem to grasp how someone who sought to unify the people under one Spirit could be the basis of such division. There were some things I didn't understand, and quite frankly, it made me uncomfortable.

Over the course of American history, it appears the role and significance of black people has been written out of the history books. With the exception of chattel slavery, their place in American history has been dismissed. One day, while at lunch with coworkers (most of whom were white), a conversation started about everyone's ancestry. It appeared everyone knew about their ancestry except for the two black people in the group. One guy was Polish and could tell you all about his family's lineage. So could the others. As they continued to rattle off their family histories and origins, there was a great level of discomfort with my black friend and me. Other than the fact we were descendants of slaves, there was little else known. To make matters worse, I really didn't know anything about my father's or mother's families here in the U.S. Sure, I had met my father's family over the years. But because there was less than a solid relationship between us when I was growing up, it was a piece of foreign history to me. As for my mother's family, I had spent a considerable amount of time around them growing up. I had cousins all over the country. However, the person I knew as my maternal grandfather may not have been my mother's birth father, thereby limiting my knowledge of that side of my family, too. Therefore, I couldn't make the claim I knew my family's ancestry.

For many African-Americans, the extent of their family knowledge begins with someone being a slave. But, not only is there a large piece of their ancestry predating slavery, there is often the in-between information eluding them as well. It's easily said, based on our skin color and physical features, we're from Africa. But this, unfortunately, paints everyone with such a broad brush that it negates and omits any specifics about our lineage and our identity. In some cases, this may not be completely true for all, as not all slaves came from Africa. Besides, Africa is a continent; a very large one, I might add. Limiting our ancestry to an entire continent gives very little information about who we are and where we have come from. That's similar to looking at someone from New Delhi, then referring to them as an Asian and expecting them to be okay with it. Technically, you would be correct as New Delhi is in India, which is on the continent of Asia. However, to do so would easily miss a significant part of who that person is and where they come from. There is a specific culture in New Delhi, and to dismiss or omit that would be a grave misunderstanding of the person and their heritage. Not to mention, that would be utterly disrespectful.

This is the context and paradigm where many African-Americans sit. Just like there is a specific culture in New Delhi, there were also specific cultures in the various countries and locales of Africa. However, many of these specifics have been lost through slavery. Any cultural aspects that may have made it through slavery can't be truly linked to one person's lineage versus another's. Therefore, we accept general aspects of what has been considered a part of the broader African culture and attach it to all black people. And since many of us have gone most of our lives seeking cultural significance, we often turned to the black church to provide us with that level of acknowledgement our American culture has historically refused to give us. Unfortunately, this has also been the case within the Church at large, which has historically omitted blacks from participating in larger Christian circles. So, black Christians have been forced to build their biblical significance from extracting bits of Old Testament scripture.

The building of black biblical significance begins in the tenth chapter of Genesis. After the flood, Ham—one of Noah's sons---settles in the lands in what is today's Africa. Ham had

four sons—Cush, Mizraim, Put, and Canaan—all who settled
in African lands. Cush and his family settled in modern-day
Sudan and Ethiopia; Mizraim in Egypt; and Put in Libya and
other lands throughout Africa. For this, Ham is often regarded
as the "Father of the Black Race." Let me first say, to limit
Ham's patriarchal contribution to one defined by the skin color
of a particular people is less than appropriate. Besides, there is
little scriptural evidence to the appearance of Ham or his sons.
In Hebrew, the name Ham means hot or warm. However, many
have said that in Egyptian, Ham means dark, and thus opted for
this as a definitive description of his racial ethnicity. However,
the Bible does not directly substantiate this statement.

Even if we decide to go along with this thinking, this is still
not a definitive indication that all things Negro belong to Ham
and all things Ham belong to the Negro, as many may lead us
to believe. Now, let me clarify something here. While I think
the focus on Ham is not theologically or spiritually appropriate,
I do recognize its initial social significance. I do recognize the
emphasis of Ham and the black race was initiated as a defensive mechanism by blacks to combat segregationist and bigoted
theology presented to promote their separation and inferiority
by many white Christian leaders.

The same scriptural passages used to defend and support the
significance of the black Christian were initially used improp-
erly to subject them to realms of continued inferiority. In the
ninth chapter of Genesis, Ham is rebuked by his brothers for
disrespectfully mocking his father—Noah—as he lay drunk
and naked. Some have said Ham was engaged in a carnal act
with his father. But again, there is no *biblical* evidence to suggest this is the case. However, there was some form of satisfaction from seeing Noah in this state, which was considered
disrespectful. Later, aware of Ham's disrespect, Noah curses
Ham's youngest son—Canaan. Because Canaan was a descen-
dent of Ham, many have referred to this as a curse against Ham.
In the curse, Noah says Canaan's future will be one of servitude

to his brothers. Since many have deemed Ham as the "father of the black race," they have also incorrectly used this passage to justify the slavery of black people. However, it is important to note this curse is not a curse against Ham or against the black race, but Canaan.

Secondly, this curse must be seen in the context of patriarchal blessings and curses seen in the Bible. Prior to death, fathers in biblical times often prophesied over the lives of their sons and their sons' descendants. Here, Noah curses Canaan. That is, he merely gives a negative announcement of Canaan's descendants that they would demonstrate the same tendency for immorality as Ham.[20] It has been speculated since Ham was Noah's youngest son, Canaan—Ham's youngest son— would be subject to the curse Noah uttered. Also, we must remember while Genesis is a historical book, it must be understood according to the context and purpose in which it was written. That is, for the purposes of setting the introduction and drawing a correlation between God and the children of Israel. The emphasis on Canaan here also serves as an opportunity for us to understand the basis of Israel's relationship with the Canaanites, whom they were to oust once they arrived at "The Promised Land." Therefore, this curse has absolutely nothing to do with anyone's skin color. In fact, such teachings are completely absurd. So, to accept this as an aspect of the black biblical cultural identity is completely wrong. I get it. The announcement of Ham as the "father of the black race" gives us significance. But how much significance does it truly give us, when the idea itself is spiritually and theologically insignificant?

So, what does all of this talk about Ham, Canaan and black people have to do with Jesus? It is motivated by the same intentions. The only difference is the discussion of Ham is generated from Old Testament scripture, while the *Jesus (ethnicity) debate* has primarily been rooted in New Testament narrative— Revelation 1:14-15. Again, I get it. The reliance on Jesus' skin being black provides a positive defense to those who sought to use scripture to separate and subject blacks to a place of inferiority. It provides significance to a people who otherwise struggled to find it. How great would one feel if they saw in themselves the same characteristics of the Messiah, the Savior of the world? Even if someone tried to subject me to feelings of inferiority, as long as my eyes are stayed on Jesus (and Jesus looks like me), I can overcome any feelings of insignificance. Trust me, I understand. But just as it is completely unacceptable to accept or attach the curse of Canaan and its negative effects to a particular racial group, it is equally as inappropriate for that same racial group to incorrectly use scripture to attach itself to particular positive characteristics for the sake of elevating themselves to a more positive position of self-worth. Again, I understand. And in this case, the debate of Jesus' skin color is just as insignificant, as it completely contradicts and under-mines his ultimate purpose. Unfortunately, residue from these teachings still exist among white and black Christians today.

Recently, my wife and I needed some minor repair work to our home. On this particular morning, a young black guy in his upper thirties arrived at my door, ready for a normal day's work. For the sake of this story, let's call him David. As he walked through our home, taking inventory of the work to be completed, David noticed several theology books in my office and began to ask me about my faith. I am never hesitant to share with someone my faith or my testimony. So, there was no way I would begin to hold back with him. His questions were intentional and pointed, as if he was struggling with some spiritual realities.

"When did you decide you wanted to go into ministry? What made you accept your call to be a pastor? How is it being a young black pastor?" The questions kept coming. At an appro-priate time, I proceeded to inquire about his spiritual journey. It turns out David was from northern Louisiana, which isn't surprising, because we're located hours west of the Louisiana state line. But as David continued sharing with me his personal spiritual journey, he proceeded to tell me he was...Mormon. Whoa! Now, that took me totally by surprise. Baptist or some Pentecostal denomination, I would expect. In fact, I would have even expected him to identify with Catholicism, as certain parts of Louisiana have dense Catholic populations. But Mormon? Never in a million years would I have guessed this young black man would have said he was Mormon. Unable to hide my surprise and curiosity, David began to express that although he had grown up Mormon, he was currently struggling to identify with Mormonism. Hence, this would explain his intense questioning.

For years, Mormons, beginning with Brigham Young, banned blacks from the priesthood. They taught blacks were cursed with dark skin because of the sins of Cain. Other Mormon authorities even taught blacks were cursed because they sided with Lucifer in his rebellion against God. Along with these theories, Mormon teaching also accepted theories the black race was cursed through Ham. It wasn't until 1978 that the ban of black priests was lifted from the Mormon Church. However, lifting this ban was simply a restatement of its policies and no real explanation of the policies of their past leaders. Unfortunately, a culture of discrimination was already established and perpetuated for more than 100 years. Prior to 1978, the racist rhetoric didn't just subject blacks to second-class citizenship within the Mormon Church, but also disqualified them from experiencing certain glories in the afterlife.

I don't use this example of Mormonism to ignite a debate on their theology or Christian acceptance. However, I do bring it up to illustrate the bigotry behind such teachings, not solely restricted to Mormons. So, although their priestly ban of blacks was lifted in 1978, it still did not deal with the overarching culture established and the effects of that culture. So, when David began to express his spiritual struggles, I understood where he was coming from.

"So why are you struggling spiritually?" I asked.

"As a black man, I find it hard to continue to associate with the Mormon Church," he began. "For years, they taught blacks were cursed. And even though they allow blacks, I still feel people look at me as if I am cursed. So, it doesn't feel like I am a brother, but rather, a project or a charity case." David went on to express the hurt he had experienced. For most of his life, he was committed and gave to the Mormon church. He had been a foreign missionary. He willingly served in other areas of the church. But in all of that, he still felt he wasn't welcomed; just merely tolerated. "I don't see how any black person can be associated with that church," he continued. "To stay there, I have to lie to myself and simply say although I don't believe the inherent teachings, this *particular* church is true," he said.

As he continued, I could feel his hurt. David was now eagerly seeking an experience with the black church and Black Jesus. For David and many other blacks, the confusion of their heritage serves as an indictment on their future. If my future is cursed, what does that say about my destiny? And if my destiny is also cursed, what's the point of fighting a losing battle? David then walked away with the assumption that what he needs is a Jesus who will make him feel good about his heritage and his destiny. A Jesus who understands him. A Jesus who knows what he has been through. A Jesus who...looks like him. Black Jesus.

PART 2 – THE SEARCH

DADDY, I LIKE WHITE BOYS

O ne thing I like doing is listening to other people's stories. I find it interesting to hear what others have gone
through. By listening to others' stories, you can understand so
much about them. What makes them sad, what brings them joy,
and what lessons they have learned along the way. So, when
I sat down for a recent conversation with one of my white
pastor friends, I was very curious to hear his story. Normally,
I wouldn't specify the racial background of the person I'm
referring to. However, for the sake of this discussion, it's relevant. Pastor Rock (as I often call him) and I always seemed
to enjoy having *real* conversations with one another. Although
he's much older than I am, he's just a cool guy who, like me,
desires to lead people to an experience with God and who's not
afraid to share with anyone the many mistakes he's made in his
life. It's always pleasant hanging out with him.

Recently when we got together, Pastor Rock shared with
me how God delivered him from the rocker lifestyle of drugs
and alcohol many years ago. His testimony is nothing short
of impressive, as I'm sure it would inspire the least of us.
Listening to his story, I curiously asked him about his earlier
experiences with the black church and the white church as they
relate to blacks. This line of questioning could have gotten
uncomfortable very quickly. However, given the rapport that

we had established, I took the risk. Besides, I'm not that sensitive to get very touchy about racial and cultural matters, and based on my experience, I didn't think he was either. And even though it's not a line of questioning I am sure many people inquire about, he didn't hesitate in being very open and honest with me about his experiences.

As he recalled, he spent years rocking out in a travelling band and experiencing every bit of the stereotypical rock and roll lifestyle. One day, feeling the effects of the previous night's activities, Pastor Rock had what many of us in Christian circles call a "Damascus Road Experience." He experienced the power of God over his body and the love of God in his heart. He then invited Jesus to be the Lord of his life, and since has been totally delivered from drugs and alcohol. With no special treatments or rehabilitation programs, God delivered him from the rocker lifestyle and restored his health. He quickly got involved with his local church in Virginia and began to serve with the pastor there.

After years of serving, he noticed an apparent absence of people of color within their congregation. Some would say he was being naïve, but I choose to believe God was imparting something in him and positioning him for the work he is doing within his ministry today. Nevertheless, he sought answers. When Pastor Rock asked about the absence of blacks within their ministry, the senior pastor of the church dismissively responded, "If we let them in our churches, they will then begin marrying our daughters." And there it was. The pastor of a sizeable Virginian congregation preaching about the loving God, but unwilling to demonstrate that same love and openly worship with others out of fear they may "marry *their* daughters."

Now, in all fairness, let me paint the context of this picture. This conversation took place in the mid-1970s. In fact, it was slightly before I was born in 1977, and only years after interracial marriages became legal (1967) in the United States. In fact, Alabama became the last state to legally accept interracial marriages in 2000. So socially, I understand the country was in an interesting place at that time. While integration of blacks and whites began to take place socially, if they could help it, many were committed to doing their part to ensure it didn't bleed into the realms of the home or go any further than what was legally necessary. So, while they couldn't deliberately prevent blacks from their worship experiences, they weren't exactly trying to send open invitations either. And God forbid if unified worship experiences led to interracial marriage.

In the previous chapter, I spoke of the Mormon perpetuation of their resistance to blacks within their spiritual circles. Interracial marriage was also a grave sin taught within Mormon circles. Mormon leader, Brigham Young expressed the sinfulness of interracial marriage by suggesting the only way one could make amends for such a sin was to have his "head cut off."[21] Again, I include the example of Mormons in this discussion to illustrate the pervasiveness of such thoughts and ideologies. But although the 1970s saw several religious denominations and groups begin to relax their positions on black participation and black leadership in the church, there still existed an underlying fear and desire to keep the cultures separate. And it wasn't just limited to the white fear of blacks. As a kid, I also experienced the effects of this same fear as it existed within black communities as well.

From my teen to my young adult years, I was proudly considered a ladies' man. Like most inner-city boys, the primary topics on my mind were sports and girls. In fact, girls often occupied the number one spot on my priority list. I can remember often being referred to as "mannish," which at the time, I took great pride in. Interestingly, I don't ever remember my mother really discouraging me from being so girl crazy. Since she was a single mother and didn't really know how to raise young men, she considered my hormonal crazes a typical phase of young men. So instead of discouraging it, she simply gave my brothers and me three essential rules we needed to adhere to when it came to dating.

One: she would say, "I am not raising a whore house." Excuse my candor, but my mother didn't sugarcoat it. This was the first rule of dating in the King household. This was her way of telling us that we were to have a certain level of respect and decorum. We were to always be respectful of her and the women we brought home. She also emphasized the young women we were allowed to see needed to operate with the same level of respect and dignity.

Two: "I'm not raising any babies," she often recited. Teenage pregnancy has been a social concern for years, and my mother made it quite evident that if we thought we were responsible enough to do what it takes to make a baby, we would need to be responsible enough to raise the baby. And while I was familiar with several of my friends and associates who experienced the struggles of teenage pregnancy, I am fortunate enough to say my brothers and I never fell into this category.

While the third rule was preached to us from our early dating years, it didn't possess any relevance until I graduated high school and went to college. As a teen, every aspect of my environment was centered on the black social experience. My school, church and neighborhood were all predominantly black. So, when I made the decision to attend college in Des Moines, Iowa—a state not known for its black population—my mother didn't hesitate to remind me on a daily basis of the third and final rule of dating in the King household: "Don't bring no white girls home." To emphasize her point, she would add, "If she can't use your comb, don't bring her home (referring to the difference in hair texture between whites and blacks)."

Now you may recall me discussing the paradigm from which my mother saw the world. Again, my mother grew up in Vicksburg, Mississippi in the mid-1940s. This was a time when racial tensions in the south were at their peak. It was a time where black men would be killed and tortured for even showing the slightest interest in a white woman. For example, the famous case of Emmett Till being lynched because he allegedly flirted with a white woman took place in Mississippi in 1955. My mother grew up in a place and time where blacks were often threatened and fearful of death if they "stepped out of their place." To say there was racial injustice would be nothing more than a severe understatement. And unfortunately, these memories were still far too fresh in her mind. So, for her, warning me of dating outside of the black culture was an attempt to save my life. And if there was any rule she was adamant about, this was it.

Fortunately, her reality and experience were not mine. Sure, I experienced my share of racism and discrimination. But it was nothing like what my mother would have experienced during her childhood. And since my truth didn't align with her truth, there was an element of rebellion I would display when it came to this rule in particular. So, in all of her warnings, I would merely oblige her by jokingly stating, "Okay, Ma. You will never *catch* me with a white girl," which we both knew meant I would simply respect her wishes and not disrespect her home, as she had literally caught me in compromising situations with other women in the past. Besides, for me to pursue a relationship with White Jesus and not experience the love of those who White Jesus created was oxymoronic.

Let me pause and clarify something here. While my mother expressed this as one of her rules, I am totally convinced that if I made the decision at that time to date and/or marry a woman of another culture, my mother would have supported my decision. Her relationship with us was always one of concern. She saw it as her purpose to provide us with opportunities she did not have and to protect us from the dangers she faced. This was her way of doing just that. However, this story illustrates how the residue of the past can be passed down to future generations, thereby restricting a move of God to unify His people, which even further emphasizes my point of why socially I believe we are in a time now that is ripe for the people of God to come together with one voice.

In an article titled, "Interracial Marriage in the U.S. Climbs to New High, Study Finds," the Huffington Post states, "Interracial marriages in the U.S. have climbed to 4.8 million – a record 1 in 12 – as a steady flow of new Asian and Hispanic immigrants expands the pool of prospective spouses. Blacks are now substantially more likely than before to marry whites."[22] When it comes to dating and marital relationships, we are progressively seeing a time where fewer people are concerned with the sociological and cultural barriers that existed a few decades ago and are more concerned with, as Martin Luther King, Jr. put it, "the content of one's character." Where social convention may have erected barriers, technology has opened doors as more and more people are finding it easier to engage in activities that were once considered taboo. In my mother's day, to initiate a relationship with a white woman would have meant death for a young black man. But today, there are Internet sites tailored to those specifically open to dating people of other cultures. So, the experiences of the older generations are no longer the experiences of the younger. Younger generations are more accepting of other cultures and more welcoming to experiences with people who don't necessarily look like them. It's the experience of love and acceptance they seek, not the safety and protection of being with someone who looks like them.

This became even more of a reality to me during a conversation with my oldest daughter. One day, she came to me in all of her cuteness with a confession she wanted to finally come clean about.

"Daddy," she said in her cute, squeaky voice. Anyone who knows me knows how I light up when I interact with my daughters.

"Yes," I responded. Although it was the end of a long day, I wanted her to know she had my full and undivided attention.

"I have a confession to make," she responded.

"Uh oh," I thought. Hearing this from your child is just as nerve-wracking as hearing, "We need to talk" from your spouse. You don't know what's on the other end of that phrase, but you're more than certain it's not anything good. Hearing those words from my daughter sent chills down my spine. My mind began racing. Nowadays, it could be anything. Peer pressure. Bullying. She could have broken something. It could have been anything. And my mind seemed to race through all the good and bad thoughts you could imagine in about two seconds. I don't even think I had the nerve to ask her what her confession was. I think she just saw I was uneasy and just decided to voluntarily relieve me of my mental torture.

So, she just blurted it out, "I like white boys."

"Whew," I thought. Wanting to be sure I heard her correctly, I responded with the usual, "Huh?" as if I hadn't heard her.

"You heard me," she said. "I like white boys."

At the time, my daughter was just nine years old. Of course, there was the whole issue of her liking boys at such an early age. But I didn't want to focus on that thing and miss what was being revealed to me in the moment. And I must admit, this was a completely new experience for me. And seeing I hadn't read the section that covered this particular situation in the *Black Parent's Handbook,* I was completely clueless as to how to respond. So, I relied on my instinct and simply burst into laughter. That's right. I literally fell over laughing. Even now, I think it's the funniest thing. My response totally took her by surprise. She never expected me to respond so hysterically to such a serious statement.

After several minutes of hearing me cackle like a hyena, she finally asked, "Daddy, what's so funny?"

"I don't know, Sweetie," I answered. I still don't know what was so funny. Maybe it was the instant recollection of the unheeded warnings given to me by my mother. Or perhaps it was the silly smile she displayed as she told me. Whatever it was, I was completely tickled. "That's great, Sweetie," I said.

We continued talking for several minutes. She told me about the particular young boy she had eyes for, and also proceeded to ask me about my interracial dating experiences. Albeit, the conversation was somewhat uncomfortable, especially since this was one of the first times my princess had come to me about boys. But even in its awkwardness, it taught me so much about the change between the past and current social climate and how that change now serves as a ripe opportunity for a move of God to erase the color line within the Church and in society-at-large.

Unlike my mother, my daughter is growing up in a society that, for the most part, embraces integration within our personal lives. She lives in a neighborhood with whites, blacks, Hispanics, and Asians. She plays on recreational teams with people of varying cultures. Her school can be described as a coat of many colors. And several of her cousins are of mixed race. This is vastly different from what I was exposed to, and even more different from what my mother experienced in Mississippi. Her experience will not be mine, as mine wasn't my mother's. Therefore, in the midst of her confession, the one thing I was sure to do was to not project the effects of my experience or my mother's onto her. At this point, she possesses a certain level of innocence that would be criminal for me to alter. I love my mother very much. But I must say she was wrong to project the pain of her experience onto us. It merely perpetuated a spirit of fear and division, neither of which are of God. So, when my daughter came to me with her confession, behind my response was the joy of a proud father. But even more so, there was the joyful expectation of a Kingdom citizen to see the illustration of God's kingdom here on earth.

As I mentioned earlier, I grew up in a predominantly black environment. Everything about my childhood centered on the black experience. So, it was a complete culture shock when I went to college in Iowa, a state largely known for its lack of black people. In fact, when I tell people I went to college in Iowa, I always get the same question: "What made you decide to go to there?" For nearly two decades since I graduated college, I always received the same question. But the truth is, I wanted to get as far away from home as possible. Seriously. I wanted new experiences. I knew the real world was not made up of all black people. I wanted to understand other cultures. I wanted to be able to effectively communicate, interact with and understand others who didn't look like me. I guess God put that desire in me for such a time as this.

In the spring semester of my junior year of college, I decided to take a course titled, *The Sociology of the African-American Experience*. For starters, the professor teaching the course had to have been the coolest professor on the face of the earth. And secondly, a course like this was definitely an opportunity for me and the other black students taking the course to let the white students know just what it was like to be black. The course covered everything from African-American history to the emergence of hip hop music. But the most intense discussions were on interracial dating. These intense discussions often lasted much longer than the specified meeting period of the course, and often spilled into the halls of the student center. I will never forget the intensity experienced during one of these moments.

During the other topics in the course, the black students often presented a unified front. We all had the same views, similar experiences and related prejudices. However, this topic of interracial dating drew so much ire and created so much division, it was scary. A large percentage of the students (black men and white women) were in favor of interracial *dating* relationships. It appeared the white women were overtaken by their curiosity about black men, and the black men were tempted by the mystique of white women. However, the black women and white men were more adamant about not crossing those racial lines. Included in the group who wanted to maintain the racial barrier, was our professor. As she presented her views, she would say, "Love is not a sociological experiment." By this, she meant during that time, our society proved it was not yet ready to accept such a phenomenon.

The backlash many interracial couples faced at that time still, in many ways, threatened their livelihoods. So, even though legally interracial relationships were accepted, sociologically, they weren't. Like my mother, this professor saw things through the social construct of the south, because she was from Oklahoma and often saw the negative results of these two cultures merging. From that paradigm, safety was much more important than "love." Therefore, for her, love was not to be a sociological experiment forcing society to accept something it wasn't quite ready to adopt. While I may have been more prone to understand my professor's thought process at that time (in the 1990s), nearly twenty years later, I must emphatically disagree.

As I illustrated earlier, interracial marriages have been and continue to be on a sharp rise. A recent survey shows 50 percent of Millennial Americans approve of interracial marriage. This is a sharp increase from the 33 percent of Baby Boomers (Fig. 9.1).[23]

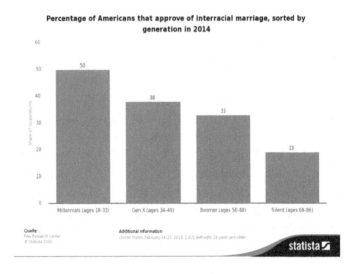

Percentage of Americans that approve of interracial marriage, sorted by generation in 2014

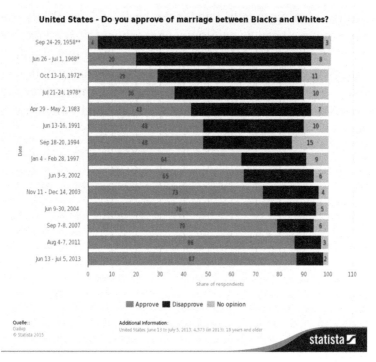

United States - Do you approve of marriage between Blacks and Whites?

In 1958, only 4 percent of American adults approved of marriage between blacks and whites. In 2013, that number was a whopping 87 percent (Fig. 9.2).[24] As we say in the south, "Times are a-changin'." Society has become more accepting of such intermingling. Our children have been exposed to much more integration than we were. Unfortunately, the only times many of them are exposed to segregation is still on Sunday mornings. While the rest of the country and the world are beginning to embrace integration into the various personal spheres of life, the Church continues to remain on the outside of that trend. I am not saying that the Church should become trendy and embrace the various sociological trends of the world.

However, "love is not a sociological experiment" is less true today, but still remains to have weight within the Church. It appears the rest of the world has been driving toward an image the Church was illustrating centuries ago. That is, various cultures coming together under the basis of *love*. While love may not have been a sociological experiment, it *is and should always be* an ecclesiastical one. It is something that should be witnessed, explored, demonstrated, and perpetuated within the Church. The recent acceptance of interracial marriages indicates the world is socially ready for a spiritual unification in the name of Love.

THE ECCLESIASTICAL
EXPERIMENT

In the previous chapter, I closed by stating in the Church, love is and should always be an ecclesiastical experiment. By this, I mean love should be the foundation from which we model and illustrate the Kingdom of God. It should be the basis of what brings us together in unity. I use the term *experiment* because it should serve as the foundation for us discovering a life unknown. That is, a life of joy, peace, and unity. For much of society, this way of life may seem foreign. But for the Church, it should be a normal way of life. Unfortunately, throughout history, this has not been the case, as the Church has taken its cues from the world and thus allowed the world's divisions to take root as weeds infiltrating its intended lush landscape.

Earlier, we saw that more than ever, cultures are coming together under the name of love. But one could argue that even though this may be true, it has provided very little change or positive effect to society-at-large. For many, the increase in interracial marriages has proven to have little effect on curbing racial biases and tensions existing in society. I hate to throw another statistic at you, but in an earlier survey by the Pew Research Center, in 2011, 44 percent of people believed an increase in interracial marriage provided no societal impact at all (Fig. 10.1).[25] While there has been an increased acceptance of interracial marriage, it also highlights many people's belief that it ultimately has had no positive effect sociologically. Yes, being involved in an interracial marriage can provide an opportunity for people to expand their knowledge of a particular culture. But until that expanded understanding spills into the throes of society and changes how the cultures deal with one another, then it can be argued that it has little to no positive effect.

We don't have to resort to statistics to question the positive effect interracial marriages have had on society overall. Read a recent magazine, newspaper article, or watch any television news station and you can witness the heightened racial and cultural tensions taking place in America and across the globe. In fact, at the time of this writing, racial tensions have been on the rise throughout the United States as several blacks have been killed at the hands of white law enforcement officers. Even with the elevation of interracial marriage, it appears we continue to battle the effects of the racial and cultural divide.

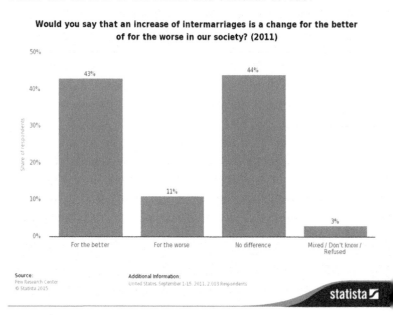

Would you say that an increase of intermarriages is a change for the better of for the worse in our society? (2011)

Source:
Pew Research Center
© Statista 2015

Additional Information:
United States, September 1-15, 2011, 2,003 Respondents

statista

So why are we talking so much about interracial marriage? And what does this have to do with erasing the color line within the Church? Let me first say, I am not saying the Church needs to overtly endorse interracial marriage to erase its color line. If it does what it was created to do, such a public endorsement would never be necessary as there would be no color line to erase. Furthermore, it's important we understand the color line is not the issue. It's merely an effect of a greater issue—an absence of Love. You see, we have been talking about interracial marriage simply because it speaks to one of the most basic needs and emotions of humans. That is, love.

Interracial marriages have been on the constant rise for years, all in the name of love. Love is a basic human emotion and need. Parallel this with the two greatest commandments for the Church, which are to love God and to love our neighbor (Mark 12:28-31). Again, the key word here is *love*. So, our discussion of interracial marriage has been merely to create a tie between the increased racial tolerance we are witnessing in the world and the intended unification we desire in the Church. At the foundation of cultural integration and spiritual unification, we see the commonality of love. But didn't we point out that although there has been an increase in interracial marriage, there has been little positive effect on society-at-large? If that's the case, why pursue this discussion any further? If unification of people in marriage has not provided any true sociological impact, what would such unification do for the Church, or society? To answer these questions, let's go a little further.

It's true. Interracial marriages have increased, all in the name of love. I acknowledged it is widely believed this phenomenon has had little to no positive impact on society-at-large. But that's because it was never intended to be the catalyst to change society. An increase in interracial marriage was simply to be one of the many positive effects of the color line being erased in the Church. This would have then produced the positive social impact so many desire and the world needs. In other words, an end became the means. Because what was intended to be an end (cultures coming together in unity) became the means, it could only produce very limited results and little positive social impact. Interracial marriage and cultural integration were never meant to be the means to unification and love. But, it was Love that led us to experience cultural integration and spiritual unification.

"Didn't you say love was at the foundation of interracial marriage?" you may ask. Yes, I did and I still stand by that statement. However, the need to be loved is different from the desire to give Love. Although love is involved, the objects where the love is directed are a critical difference. Let me explain.

As a pastor, I have the privilege of speaking with many couples during their periods of elation. When they're courting or engaged to be married, they never hesitate to tell me how much they're *in love*.

"Why do you want to marry him?" I will ask.

"Because I'm *in love* with him," the woman often says, as she proceeds to tell me how the particular guy makes her feel.

"Why do you want to marry her?" I will ask the gentleman.

"Because I love her to death," he often says.

On a side note, be careful what you say, because in marriage there are many times you will feel like the very person you love *to death* will be the cause of yours. Just kidding. At this point, though, the couple is totally smitten with one another and completely *in love*.

This idea of being *in love* is quite popular. I admit, there have been several times in my life I made similar statements. However, a major concern is that this statement indicates an alternative. If you can be *in love*, then you can also be *out of love*. Interestingly, I have come to realize when a person talks about being *in love* with someone, what they usually mean is their partner's actions generally make them feel good about themselves, their current set of circumstances, and additionally gives them hope their euphoric feeling will continue. Thus, they have strong positive feelings toward this person. Because of how this person makes them feel, they can also feel comfortable in feeling good about them. These good feelings now create an avenue in which one can (and often does) choose to demonstrate what they perceive to be loving behaviors and actions to the other.

However, instead of the actions demonstrating love the way the other party desires, it is often demonstrated in the manner the giver sees fit. Both parties will engage in this process until the positive feelings stop. As long as the memory bank is filled with memories and thoughts yielding more positive than negative feelings, they are usually good and *in love*. But as soon as the tide begins to turn, so does their love narrative. Unfortunately, since many of us have been conditioned to focus more on negative thoughts than positive ones, a problem ensues. Once this takes place, their partner no longer makes them feel good about themselves or their situation and they have very little hope of any improvement. Thus, the alternative: they are no longer *in love*.

The above scenario is what takes place when one has a strong desire *to be loved and to find the love they desire*. There is nothing wrong with having a desire to be loved. As I said before, it's a basic human need. But we must make sure the true nature of our need doesn't become lost and misunderstood in the passions of our pursuits to fulfill that very need. The whole notion of being *in love* is often dependent upon the feelings generated by the actions of the other. Therefore, it reveals the selfish nature of this kind of love. The ultimate object of this love is directed to oneself. It's one that's based on the benefit a person experiences from another, rather than the value the other has, regardless of their actions or the feelings their actions create. It says, "As long as you can continue to make me feel great about myself and my life, I love you. But if you can't, I won't love you anymore." This love is based on the expectation that someone else is responsible for your happiness and joy.

Unbeknownst to them, many individuals make a vow to make their spouses happy or die trying. And unfortunately, that's what typically happens. They die trying. So, what does this have to do with interracial marriage? This is the same type of love typically at the foundation of most marriages and relationships, including interracial ones. The primary difference is the individuals have become comfortable enough with other cultures to expand their love search into the relationship pools of those cultures they are comfortable with. And once found, they reap its various benefits.

When the pressures of life arrive, coupled with the additional social pressures arising in many interracial marriages, the benefits become short-lived. The marriage thus becomes an avenue for the individuals to experience and feel love. Sadly, it rarely (if ever) meets those expectations because it was never intended for that purpose. Again, love was never intended to be the end. It was intended to be the means to the end. Due to the selfish nature of the love that initiated the relationship, there is no avenue for the social surroundings of the couple to be positively impacted. When all roads lead to you, there is no way the society can be impacted by the love you experience. This is not just the case with interracial marriages, but most marriages.

On the other hand, the Church was called to impact society through Him who is Love. At the center of Jesus' ministry was Love and compassion. Therefore, as the Body of Christ, the Church was to reflect Love. At its core, it was to be Love for all. Not some. Not only for those who looked like them, but for all. This Love was to be at the core of the Church and was intended to be different from the love experienced and demonstrated throughout the rest of the world. This Love was to be demonstrated, not with the intention to gain something in return, but because there was such an over-abundance of it and it would be freely given to all wanting to experience it. Unlike the previous version of love we discussed, this Love was not based on the benefit received by its giver. Instead, it was centered on the true value of its recipient.

When I began my corporate career, I went through business sales training. During this training, they introduced us to a concept called the F.A.B. Sales Technique. This technique suggests when selling something to someone, you should specify the *features*, *advantages* and *benefits* of the product/service you are selling. This has inadvertently become the method by which many of us have assessed all of our relationships. Romantic, familial, cordial and professional relationships often are driven by this method. We assess the skills and features of the person with whom we are dealing. We examine what they are bringing to the table. We then determine the advantages of those features (skills) and the benefits we expect to yield from such a relationship. Unfortunately, this again is one-sided and never takes into account who the person truly is and their value. In the sales scenario, the value of the product/service was determined by the price the other person was willing to pay for the good or service. Thus, the value or worth of the thing merely becomes limited to one's specific need at the time.

The Church, on the other hand, was called and expected to deal with others based on the value God saw in them. Their value was not to be based on the perceived needs or desires of the church people. It was to be based on the price Jesus would pay for them, which we have seen was the ultimate price—his life. Therefore, the value placed on each person should be congruent with the value of Christ's life. Regardless of their flaws, blemishes, or differences, they were still to be held with the utmost value and regard. This is the kind of Love Jesus demonstrated when he forgave the adulterous woman (John 8), when he healed the centurion's servant (Luke 7), and when he healed the man with leprosy (Matthew 8), to name a few. The Church was to operate with this very same kind of Love. It was this type of Love that would serve as a catalyst to transform the social landscape as it did during Jesus' time.

95

I recently had an enlightening discussion with a black friend of mine (Lance), who happens to be married to a white woman. Lance grew up in a single-parent home in a pretty diverse Dallas suburb. His childhood church experience was largely black. Like many black children, Lance became engaged in sports to stay out of trouble while his mother often worked multiple jobs. Although he played many sports, he began to excel in soccer. While his mother worked, Lance spent many hours with his teammates' families, most of whom were white Christians. Fortunately, these families accepted him and often loved him as if he were one of their own.

As he got older, his athletic abilities offered opportunities for him to travel the world and gain an appreciation for all cultures, and he continued to experience nothing but love from those he encountered. As Lance's exposure and comfort with other cultures increased, so did his pool for dating relationships. The love he experienced from these cultures served as a seed, germinating and producing the same love to others he would encounter as an adult. Unlike me, Lance didn't have others perpetuating their fears and racial concerns onto him. What he was exposed to was a love for all.

It was this love for all that led to a beautiful marriage and family. While he is married to a woman of a different racial background, this is not something he intentionally sought out. As he puts it, "It was merely coincidental timing." It just so happened when he was ready to get married, the woman he fell in love with was of a different racial background. This is a result of having the seeds of Love being deposited into you, therefore producing the fruit of Love. This Love allows you to have compassion and see the value in others, instead of merely recognizing benefit from them. It's a Love intent on giving and less concerned with receiving. It is the Love of God. It's the Spirit of God.

I mentioned earlier a switch had taken place. At some point, the end mistakenly became the means. That is, social interracial integrations became the means. It's been no secret that racial and cultural tensions have existed throughout the world's history. A desire for social change was in place, and to satisfy the desire, cultural integration was forced upon the people. What many sought was to legally and forcefully integrate key aspects of society—education, government, and recreational living. While this gave us all exposure to one another's cultures, love was not the basis. Over time and several generations, a familiarity between the groups developed, increasing their comfort around one another. Again, foundationally, the cultural integration was forced upon a society, having no basis to truly sustain the change they were forced to undertake. Therefore, what many saw as strides in cultural unification became nothing more than simple toleration. Again, this is because cultural integration (or interracial relationships) was not to be the means to change society. They were merely to be an effect of the change society had undergone through their display of Love, which was a charge to be led by the Church. But how was the Church supposed to lead such a pursuit?

In Matthew 28:18-20, we see Jesus giving final instructions to his disciples. This is known as the Great Commission which is also the basic instruction to the Church of today.

> [18] And Jesus came and spoke to them, saying, "All authority has been given to Me in heaven and on earth. [19] Go therefore and make disciples of all the nations, baptizing them in the name of the Father and of the Son and of the Holy Spirit, [20] teaching them to observe all things I have commanded you; and lo, I am with you always, even to the end of the age." Amen.

As you see, the instruction was to "go and make disciples *of all* the nations." I place emphasis here because to make disciples of the nations was not only to teach the nations about

Jesus orally, but it was to be living witnesses and demonstrators of what he taught and did. While Jesus would be the model for his disciples, the disciples would be models for the rest of the world. To make disciples *of the nations* also meant the disciples' actions and demonstrations would directly impact the cultures and societies of the world. They would infect and affect the various nations and cultures they were sent to transform. What would be the basis of this impact? Love.

In verse 20, Jesus tells his disciples to teach others to obey everything he had commanded them. Remember, Jesus told his disciples and others the greatest commandments were to love God and to love their neighbors (Mark 12:28-31). Love was the foundation of Jesus' life, his earthly ministry and his sacrifice. Therefore, his disciples (and the Church) were to rest their actions on this same foundation. Let's look a little further.

In Matthew 5:43-48, we see Jesus discussing love toward one's enemies in his Sermon on the Mount. Here, he is contrasting the love displayed by unbelievers with how believers should love. He emphasizes we should love everyone, including our enemies. He then concludes this section by saying, "Be perfect, therefore, as your heavenly Father is perfect." At first glance, you may not see how this relates to the Church's mandate, but it does.

Unfortunately, many have mistakenly used this passage to call for moral perfection from believers. However, in this passage, Jesus is not calling for us to be perfect in the sense we see perfection in today's context. He is not expecting us to be perfect in our actions. As he is contrasting the love of the unbeliever with the love of the believer, Jesus is calling for "completeness" or for us to be "undivided" in how we demonstrate love. In the previous verses, he highlights how unbelievers (or the rest of the world) love only those who love them. They are divided in their love. Those who love them are loved back. But those who do not love them are not loved back. But his disciples and other believers should love everyone. He is calling for an undivided, complete and *perfect* love.

In a modern context, this shows we are to love everyone; those culturally like us and those who are not. Those who are physically like us and those who are not. This was to be the foundation of the Great Commission during Jesus' day as well as today. We were commissioned to be everyday representations of Jesus by modeling what he taught and commanded. By doing this, we would be able to lead and sustain effective transformations of the societies we were a part of. We would be able to make disciples of the nations.

Unfortunately, over time, the Church has not fulfilled its charge. Any time the value of a created thing is not realized by those it was intended to impact, an alternative (or counterfeit) will emerge. We see this occurring in everyday life. For example, my wife likes to buy designer handbags. When she purchases a handbag, she pays attention to its detail. The quality of the leather or material it is made of. The quality of the stitching. Its sturdiness. She wants to make sure the handbag she selects is not only going to look good on her arm, but it will hold up and last through the years as she uses it. She wants to know it's going to support all of the junk she's going to put in it. She will even spend more money on a handbag if there's a manufacturer's guarantee on the product. This lets her know if the particular handbag is not of the utmost quality and does not hold up to the retailer's or manufacturer's claims, she can return it.

Unfortunately, not everyone values handbags as much as my wife. To others, a handbag is merely a tool to put personal things in and carry. To them, they may merely be concerned with its appearance and less about the quality or the guarantee. So, instead of paying the money for the quality of a designer handbag, they would be perfectly okay with its counterfeit. Again, the intended value of the handbag was not realized by those it was intended to impact, and counterfeit options arose. This is exactly what has taken place within the Church.

The Church was to lead the charge through Love in transforming societies experiencing cultural and spiritual unity. The value the Church was to bring was the valuable experience of Love. Through this experience, authentic cultural integration would have been a result. Unfortunately, the Church was infected by the very cultures they were sent to impact and the experience the Church served up was not of the same quality of its claims. Therefore, a counterfeit emerged.

The need and the desire were present. Throughout history, people understood the benefit of unity and even love. However, when the Church didn't provide the avenue for unity (or love), the rest of the world created their own avenues, essentially forcing cultures together with no solid sustainable foundation. This created a temporary solution in which racial toleration was achieved with very little to no positive social impact. It was the counterfeit. It was the alternative answer. Regardless of the appearance, the counterfeit will never adhere to the value or quality of the original and thus, will never gain the same result. I said it before and I will say it again: Love is and was always meant to be an ecclesiastical experiment. It was something to be modeled by the Church.

A HOUSE
(KINGDOM) DIVIDED

S hortly before I sat down to write this piece, I had the pleasure of watching the 2016 NBA Western Conference Finals
Game 7 matchup between the Golden State Warriors and the
Oklahoma City Thunder (OKC). This marquee matchup did not
disappoint, as it was filled with emotion, grit and everything
else basketball fans adore. During the NBA playoffs, teams
face off against one another in a best of seven series. The first
team to win four games goes on to the next round to face the
next opponent. Well on this night, both Golden State and OKC
had each won three games. So, this game would decide which
team would win the best of seven series and move forward to
play Lebron James and the Cleveland Cavaliers for the NBA
World Championship. So far, the series between the Warriors
and the Thunder had all the makings of a sports soap opera as
they fought it out to the very last second.

While most NBA teams possess at least one elite player,
OKC had two of the best players in the NBA in Kevin Durant
and Russell Westbrook. And Golden State, posting the best regular season record in NBA history, also showed up with their
own trio of phenomenal players in Klay Thompson, Draymond
Green, and Stephen Curry—the NBA's two-time Most Valuable
Player. On this night, several of the best basketball players in

the world met center stage to duel it out for an "all the marbles" battle.

In the first half of the game, the Thunder seemed to dominate the favored Warriors. Every shot the Warriors initially threw up seemed to bounce into the hands of the Thunder and later into OKC's basket. On several occasions within the first half of the game, the Thunder led the Warriors by double-digit margins. But no matter how bad things began to look, the Warriors kept fighting. After halftime, something changed. No longer did the Warriors keep missing shots or making mistakes on defense. It seemed after halftime, they united together and every player on their roster played a significant role in their comeback victory.

You may be asking why I have suddenly turned into a sports writer. Well, at some point during the third period of the game, it wasn't the change on the Warriors' sideline that made the difference. it was the change with the Thunder that seemed to open the door for the Warriors' victory.

Midway through the third period, the Thunder players became visibly frustrated. They saw several double-digit leads evaporate and were looking at their own hole they needed to climb out of. So, their frustration was warranted. But instead of coming together like the Warriors had done previously, they turned their frustration toward one another. They became divided and slowly imploded. You see, their defeat didn't take place when all the time ran out on the clock. It took place the moment they turned on one another instead of working together. Sure, they had some isolated good plays, but their collective effectiveness was lost in the moment of division. And because their collective effectiveness was lost, they failed to reach the objective they set out to achieve.

I use this example to illustrate this is where the Church is. And Jesus knew the results of division all too well.

In Mark 3, Jesus is accused of being possessed by Satan. In fact, his accusers claim it is with Satan's power that Jesus is able to cast out demons. As we see in his response, this logic seems absurd to Jesus, as he replies, "How can Satan drive out Satan? [24] If a kingdom is divided against itself, that kingdom cannot stand. [25] If a house is divided against itself, that house cannot stand. [26] And if Satan opposes himself and is divided, he cannot stand; his end has come... (Mark 3:24-26, NIV)."

Jesus teaches no kingdom, no organization, no entity, no family, and no individual can effectively and successfully achieve their objective if there is division within. John 17 leads us to an understanding of how important his prayer for unity was. During a majority of its existence, the American Church (and abroad) has largely been divided. We have been divided by doctrine, practices, socio-economic class, gender, and race (to name a few). There have been reports of more than 30,000 Christian denominations. While I cannot even attempt to name all of them, I am aware that several of them were formed largely because of racial divisions. Those not officially formed on the basis of racial discord somehow ended up racially segregated. Now don't get me wrong, I am not writing this text to make a universal call to end denominationalism. However, I am stating that although there may be various differences, the differences in method or appearance don't have to halt the primary objective of representing and expanding the kingdom of God. I am also stating my belief that the looming racial and cultural divide existing within the Church has all but killed our collective effectiveness and our opportunity to successfully fulfill the objective at hand.

When I look at Jesus' words, I notice something very interesting. In his response, Jesus says, "if [the enemy] opposes himself and is divided...his end *has come*." Notice he doesn't say his end will come, but it *has come,* as in it already took place. The arrival of the end is now in the past. In other words, at the point in which division has crept in, there marks the end.

But what about the racial divide? Don't our racial differences automatically divide us? The answer to this question is no. Our racial, cultural, economic and gender differences don't have to divide us. Difference does not equal division. However, if we are not careful, it can easily lead to division. In the context of race and culture, the difference is not chosen, whereas the division is. Let me explain.

I have a good friend who, for the sake of anonymity, we will call Steve. Steve is a black man. Steve's race as a black man was decided without his input. He had no say-so in the matter. When he was born, he was black. At the same time, Steve is married to a white woman—Laura. Like Steve, Laura had no input in the fact she's a white woman. At first glance, we will notice two glaring differences between Steve and Laura—their ethnicity and their gender. Now I am quite sure if we continued to explore the details of their personalities, thoughts, beliefs, fears, goals, and past experiences, we would be able to identify more differences between the two.

For now, let's just examine the two obvious differences. These are two differences completely out of their control. When they both entered into this world, they were ethnically and genetically different. Now as husband and wife, Steve and Laura are members of the same family. In fact, as husband and wife, they are committed to the common goal and purpose of expanding and establishing their respective family. Although they are different, the fact they are a part of the same family brings them together to achieve the common goal. Of course, they both may play different roles in how the goal is achieved. Nevertheless, they are united in the purpose to where their differences are of no consequence. Their race and gender are merely differences that exist. In fact, their differences are beneficial to the overarching objective.

This is how it is to be with the Church and fellow believers. Our common objective of representing the King and making disciples should supersede any cultural, racial, or gender differences that may exist. We are all to be the salt of the earth and the light of the world (Matthew 5:13-16). We have all been commissioned to make disciples of Jesus Christ. Our mission is the same. While we may have different methods, ideas and roles to play in accomplishing the mission, we are still to be united by the mission.

To be divided would be a choice. It would be a choice to pursue our own preferences, agendas and traditions over the common mission. Division operates with the idea the individual parts are greater than the whole. And when we are no longer united by the mission, we have then turned our focus from the mission to ourselves.

Historically, there have been brief moments where it appeared the color line within the American Church had been erased. These moments typically have been the result of revival movements. One in particular was during the Azusa Street Revival of 1906. The Azusa Street Revival was the launching point of Pentecostalism in the American Church. Led by William Seymour (a black man), thousands of people of various cultural, economic, social and religious backgrounds experienced an outpouring of the Holy Spirit that could be likened to Pentecost in the Book of Acts. For a little more than three years, people from all over traveled to Los Angeles to experience what God was doing at the Azusa Street Mission. Twenty-four hours a day, 365 days a year, people were being delivered, restored and healed as they experienced miraculous encounters with God.

Outside of the wonderful spiritual encounters, the Azusa Street revival was greatly noted for the interracial harmony taking place during its meetings.[26] Keep in mind, this was during a time when systematic segregation was the norm. In fact, during this time many laws were passed instilling stiff consequences for those in interracial relationships and marriages. "The interracial aspects of Azusa Street were a striking exception to the racism and segregation of the times. The phenomenon of blacks and whites worshipping together under a black pastor seemed incredible to many observers."[27] Literally, millions of church-goers today have been indirectly influenced by what took place at Azusa.

There are two reasons I bring up the movement that began at Azusa. The first is to provide historical awareness that, at some point, the color line had been washed away amongst believers. Albeit for three years, it took place during a time when segregation and division was at its peak. The second reason I bring up the Azusa Street Revival is to highlight its reasons for ending.

There has been much speculation about how the Azusa Street Revival came to its end. No matter what ideas are presented about the specific events leading to the end of this revival, the fact remains the Azusa Street Revival ended because of one thing—an overwhelming distrust developed between the leaders of the movement and their differences. In other words, there became a greater focus on the differences of opinion, the differences in protocol, differences in doctrine, and the differences in race. As key players focused on these differences, personal agendas came to the forefront, thereby overshadowing the work of God taking place.

One thing the end of this movement shows us is that God will not work in contrast to your personal objective and agenda. What we saw at Pentecost and at Azusa Street were different people coming together, united with the same desire to experience God. Because of that unified desire, God's Spirit moved upon them in such a way others wanted to also be affected by their experience. This unification in desire and Spirit opened a door for them to touch heaven from earth and affect millions. However, once the unified desire ended, so did the movement.

As long as our focus remains inward on our differences and not upward toward God, we will never see the Church have the effect on society it was called to have. We will continue to have temporary visitations providing short-lived results.

You see, Pentecost and Azusa were effective because the Spirit of God was able to move on the unified cry by the people. God moved upon them to create a noticeable difference in their lives, and people were positively affected by the ongoing changes taking place. Currently, there is not a unified cry or desire for God to move upon the believers. Instead, the Church is currently crying out for God to move, but in the process of Him moving, we want Him to be mindful of our differences. Thus, He never moves in the way that ignites sweeping social change. Because of this, the Church has lost its collective effectiveness. Sure, we have had some "good plays" and events here and there, similar to the OKC Thunder. But our overall effectiveness has been lost and will continue to be as long as we don't realize that difference is inevitable, but division is a choice.

FEARFUL LOVE

O ne Sunday morning while teaching our church congregation, I had the urge to poll the people on an important question.

"What's the opposite of love?" I asked, followed by a long silent pause. Knowing me, most of them had a feeling it was a trick question and just sat in their seats waiting for me to give them the answer. "This is not a rhetorical question," I said. "Let me hear it. Just shout it out. What's the opposite of love?" I asked again.

"Hate. Anger. Dislike. Disdain," they yelled.

"Just as I thought," I began. "We all have been taught the opposite of love is hate or some form of dislike toward a particular person or thing. But, this is not entirely the case. The opposite of love is not hate, but it is fear," I said. Instantly their eyes widened, indicating they were curious and eager to hear more. "That's right. The opposite of love is fear," I repeated.

Let's explore this a little further.

As I have gotten older, I have come to a realization most conflicts and misunderstandings are the result of some sort of fear. Think about the last conflict you had with another person. What was the cause of the offense? Perhaps it was the fear of being taken advantage of (or disrespected). Maybe it was the fear of loss or even the fear of failure. At the root of the conflict,

I am sure the initial offense was based on fear. Whether we know it or not, fear has begun to consume most of our lives. It has been the reason we do certain things and why we don't do certain things. As a young man growing up, I was consumed with fear, some of which was passed down from others, and some of it was self-initiated. Regardless of how it came about, the fact remains there was and still remains great fear that I must be intentional about overcoming. I have also witnessed growing fears in my children as they develop.

Recently, my wife came to me with an observation about our two-year-old daughter. We both noticed the older she gets, the more aware she becomes about certain things. As her awareness and her knowledge of certain things grow, so does her propensity to realize certain fears. When she was fresh out of the womb, of course, she had no fear. When she began to walk, she developed a fear of falling. And now, at nearly three years old, she verbalizes more and more fears. Fear of the dark. Fear of being left alone and a fear of dogs. Unfortunately, she hasn't quite developed the fear of getting in trouble. But in due time, I am sure it will come as well. What is disappointing in all of this is I am keenly aware that as she continues to go through life, there will be many more fears society will project on her. The fear of strangers. The fear of failure. And depending on her cultural upbringing, perhaps the fear of white (or black) people.

I mentioned a few times in this book that growing up, I was encouraged to have a natural fear of white people and the white system. It was the "Fear of the Man." The "Man" was anything associated with or representing the white establishment. After years of achieving some levels of success within the "white establishment," these fears still persist and can be seen in my interactions today. For example, as a young black male, there were several rules passed down to me that I still adhere to today when driving. Rule number one: never travel in a car full of young black men. The sight of several young black men in a car together just spelled trouble and thus made us targets for police (or white) suspicion.

Rule number two: if you get stopped by the police while driving, make sure your hands are in the ten and two positions on the steering wheel so the officer can see them. Don't make any sudden moves, because you don't want to be considered a threat. Rule number three: shut up when talking to white police officers. These rules are still followed today. But they were passed down to me out of a fear black men were unfairly targeted and victimized by white police officers. And unfortunately, it's still a concern that rightly exists today.

I mentioned earlier my mother's restriction against interracial dating was not because she hated white people. It was birthed out of a fear bad things happened to black men dating white women. Based on her experiences, I can definitely understand why she would encourage me to refrain from certain behaviors. Regardless of the justification, the root of it all is still fear.

Do I think all black people hate white people? Absolutely not. Do I think all white people hate blacks, Hispanics, or other minority groups? Certainly not. However, I do believe many are fearful of one another. And those who are somehow proud to profess a disdain for the other, I guarantee weren't born with such hatred. I am more than certain it began with some fear that was either passed down or manifested through some negative experience. I am more than certain, like my daughter, at the age of two, such a fear or hatred of the other didn't exist. It was learned.

A good question to ask is: Where is the Church in all of this? As believers in Jesus Christ, it is our responsibility to promote and perpetuate love to all we come into contact with. In John chapter 14, Jesus tells his disciples, "If you love Me, keep My commandments (John 14:15)." These commandments are not referring to the Ten Commandments or a list of '*thou-shall-nots* so many people futilely try to adhere to. These commandments are the commandments of love.

> Jesus replied: "'Love the Lord your God with all your heart and with all your soul and with all your mind.' [38] This is the first and greatest commandment. [39] And the second is like it: 'Love your neighbor as yourself.'" (Matthew 22:37-39, NIV)

This is the Church's role. It's to promote the heavenly agenda of love. But what does this look like? 1 Corinthians 13:4-8 (NIV) is a good explanation of what love is:

> [4] Love is patient, love is kind. It does not envy, it does not boast, it is not proud. [5] It does not dishonor others, it is not self-seeking, it is not easily angered, it keeps no record of wrongs. [6] Love does not delight in evil but rejoices with the truth. [7] It always protects, always trusts, always hopes, always perseveres.

> [8] Love never fails. But where there are prophecies, they will cease; where there are tongues, they will be stilled; where there is knowledge, it will pass away.

This passage does a great job of describing what love is. Later, in verse 13 of the same chapter, scripture states the greatest of faith, hope, and love, is love.

To continue, let's take a quick look at 1 John 4:18. It states, "There is no fear in love; but perfect love casts out fear, because fear involves torment." It not only illustrates there is no existence of fear in love, but it also states love has an adverse or opposite reaction to fear, driving it out. It should also be noted the term *perfect* does not mean without error or flaws. But it refers to completeness. A love is made complete and mature in Him who is Love. This complete love is a non-divisive love. It is a non-discriminating love. It is complete in theory and in practice.

As believers in Jesus Christ, we are to be led by the same Spirit Christ was led by (Romans 8:14). This is the Spirit of Love. 2 Timothy 1:7 states God has not given us (believers) a spirit of fear but one of love. The nature of Love is to give. It is to give the same gift we, ourselves, have received, which is love. It is a gift that does not have a requirement of reciprocity. Love says I give because I have Love, regardless of whether or not I am given love in return. Love comes with mercy and grace, while "fear has to do with torment (or punishment)."

Unfortunately, the Church has not operated with the Love our Scriptures encourage us to live by. We have promoted a fearful love, which by definition cannot exist. It's an oxymoron. While love gives, the nature of fear is to retreat and defend. In fear, we possess the desire to defend that which we value most. In the case of cultural diversity, what we value most is our cultural identity and cultural significance. Because fear is the root, blacks and whites alike fight to protect their cultural significance in a kingdom where you were significant long before your race or culture were ever recognized. This is what Black and White Jesus inadvertently teach. That is, to protect your blackness (or whiteness) and defend it at all costs against those unworthy intruders. It was this fear from both sides that ushered me into a spiritual whirlwind and led to my disassociation with both Black Jesus and White Jesus.

TRADING IN BLACK JESUS AND WHITE JESUS

As I've mentioned before, I spent many years in a fervent pursuit of White Jesus. To my surprise and pleasure, I eventually found him. But also—to my dismay—once I did, it wasn't all it was cracked up to be. Don't get me wrong. There were definitely some positive aspects to my experience. In fact, when I first "found" him, I could have sworn I entered heaven. But just like Black Jesus, the more time I spent with him, the more troubled I became.

If you recall, my initial search began as an attempt to escape the continuous emotions of struggle and strife perpetuated by Black Jesus and the black church. My previous experiences in the black church seemed to produce a cloudy haze of despair and an expectation the struggle would never end. It created within me a depressing spirituality I wasn't quite comfortable with. Black Jesus seemed to bring the struggle to heaven when heaven was supposed to be a place of escape. It was suffocating and I just needed to get some air—some "white air." And because of that, I will never forget the feeling I felt when I met White Jesus.

After attending many predominantly white churches of varying denominations, I apprehensively walked into a white Baptist church in Southwest Houston. By now, my search lasted

113

over a number of years, with me frequently attending white churches, while occasionally satisfying an innate yearning for the soul of the black church. However, this particular Sunday was a white church Sunday. It included all the anxiety that accompanied the previous white church Sundays. My apprehension was rooted in the fact I already attended several other (white) churches before and was met with piercing stares, clearly sending me the message that White Jesus was for whites only. But I had come too far to turn back now. I had been searching for years. Although my search thus far had turned up empty results, I just couldn't quit. Or better yet, I just couldn't return to the depressing spiritual experience I grew up with. Besides, each negative encounter just meant I was closer to a positive one. It was as if I were searching for lost treasure.

Although there was doubt resulting from the experiences of my past failures, my spiritual metal detector was beeping so loudly, I just knew I was on the brink of a satisfying discovery. So, I inquisitively walked into the large sanctuary, cordially speaking to the first friendly face that met me. The service had already begun. The lights were dimmed. The music was peaceful and familiar. People sang along with the worship band, with arms lifted in the air. As the usher led me to an open seat, the person sitting next to me greeted me with a handshake and an invitation to get comfortable, which I gladly accepted. I comfortably positioned myself in my seat and joined everyone else in worship. It was pleasant. Peaceful. A sense of calm rested upon the place as we sang contemporary Christian worship songs. It was beautiful — as if the angels themselves were singing. It may have been my imagination, but I would have sworn I saw white doves flying around the sanctuary. Like the rest of the congregation, I began to get lost in the worship as we sang of our love for God. Although we didn't sing the upbeat music I had grown accustomed to in the black church, the music didn't have the painful heaviness it had during my youth. My mother was right. The music was different. It was

114

light. Airy. And peaceful. It seemed as if everyone in the room was problem-free. In that moment, I began to feel the same way. I felt like every problem I walked in with was lifted off my shoulders. I had not one care in the world.

Shortly after the worship period, the pastor came to the podium and delivered a thirty-minute message encouraging us to push past our obstacles to success. There was no fanfare, no drawn out theatrics. It was motivating. I walked out of there feeling good about myself. I felt like there was nothing I couldn't accomplish, and it was just what I had been looking for. Eureka! I had finally done it. I finally found White Jesus, and for nearly a year, I continued to go back for a weekly appointment with my white savior.

Each meeting, I was met with similar experiences as the first. However, the peace of my Sunday morning experience rarely transferred to my Monday morning reality. While I often found some temporary relief from the black struggle on Sunday, later in the week, I was sure to return to the struggles I was so fervently seeking salvation from. At the time, White Jesus was good to me, but the fact remained, I still encountered the daily struggles of black life. Economic struggles. Struggling for significance and identity. Professional and social discrimination and degradation. Fighting to get ahead, with little to no expectation of actually doing so.

Regardless of what I faced during the week, White Jesus always seemed to come through for me on Sunday mornings. Since each encounter with White Jesus left me with good feelings about myself and my life, I decided to seek more experiences with him to combat the ill feelings of my everyday reality. I began attending midweek church services, small group Bible discussions, and several special events throughout the week. The more church events I could attend, the better. White Jesus became my drug of choice, and since he was clothed in religion, who would have thought my relationship with him would be damaging?

The more time I spent with White Jesus, the more I began to assimilate to his way of thinking. You see, White Jesus was birthed from the spirit of privilege, which is also the spirit in which he baptized his followers. Socially, this is described as "white privilege." This is the idea that white people experience various societal benefits and privileges blacks and other non-whites do not. While the notion of white privilege still remains to be debated, it appears White Jesus covertly seeks to protect this sense of privilege at all costs. Therefore, to those who are privileged, there is no such thing. There's just life. But where there is a spirit of privilege, there is a lack of empathy for others and the injustices they may face. Again, to those who are privileged or benefit from a privileged system, there is no such thing. To the underserved, there is injustice.

For people to exist in and benefit from privilege, they must be comfortable resting above those not of this system. To do so means there is a lack of empathy and compassion as one rationalizes the injustice as it is perpetuated. Sure, there may be some lightweight acknowledgment about certain struggles and injustices existing for others, but empathy—no. Privilege and empathy can't coexist. When led by a spirit of privilege, even charitable and altruistic works such as feeding the homeless, clothing drives, etc., have a self-benefitting purpose. When led by a spirit of privilege, these works are ultimately intended to make the privileged feel more comfortable with sitting high on their perch. It makes one feel good for doing a work, even if it's not what's needed to truly help the other person. When led by the spirit of privilege, the underprivileged are seldom victims, but are often the cause of their own demise.

As my time with White Jesus increased, so did my exposure to the spirit of privilege. I admit it. Being in the midst of such privilege was gratifying. It felt good. I felt accomplished. But within a year of my love affair with White Jesus, I noticed a disconnect. As my time with White Jesus increased, so did my disdain for my own people. That's right. I developed distaste for the very people I was culturally connected to. I viewed the actions of the black community from the perch of privilege. I lacked empathy for those going through some of the very struggles I escaped from. I lacked empathy for those I was associated with every day. And at some point, it all came to a head, and I was faced with a serious challenge.

While my search lasted longer, my time with White Jesus only lasted for about eighteen months. It all came to a head when I was encouraged to start my own business. I always desired to be an entrepreneur, but lack of know-how and financial resources often prevented me from making the leap. But, as I mentioned before, White Jesus was very encouraging. And taking my cue from him, I decided to make the leap into entrepreneurship. Besides, I was affiliated with White Jesus now. Call it delusional, but I seriously expected to have the favor of white people, or at least be able to tap into the "White Jesus Social & Business Network." I wasn't expecting to divinely be given good credit or anything, but I also wasn't expecting to have to fight as hard, either. Let's be real. I was affiliated with White Jesus now. I hoped that with this affiliation came open doors, opportunities, and connections I hadn't been exposed to before. As I quickly learned, however, this wasn't the case.

I had just completed classes to become a licensed real estate agent and was excited to begin my entrepreneurial endeavors. I did everything my research suggested. I received my incorporation charter from the state. I registered my business with the IRS. I had my business plan. Every suggested step, I made a point to diligently complete. I had done everything to become an official business, with the exception of establishing a business bank account. I opened several bank accounts in the past, so I was sure this would be the easiest and the most rewarding step.

On that day, I dressed in a nice gray suit with a freshly laundered, white dress shirt. I didn't want to look too formal, so I omitted the tie. This was a big day for me and I wanted to be taken seriously by the banking officer. I had my paperwork neatly placed in my leather portfolio. As we would say growing up, I was "cleaner than the Board of Health." I was ready.

When I arrived at the bank, I confidently walked into the lobby and signed in. I sat in the lobby area for about fifteen minutes, waiting for an available bank officer to call my name.

"Chris?" the bank officer finally asked.

"Yes, that's me," I said.

"Have a seat," he said, directing me to an empty seat in his office. "How can I help you?"

"Well I was told this is a good bank for business banking. So, I would like to establish a business checking account," I said, while handing him my paperwork and an initial check for several thousand dollars. Earlier, I began saving money from my corporate sales job for the purposes of starting a business. I wasn't sure what the minimum deposit requirements were for a business bank account, but I wanted to ensure I deposited more than enough to cover my basic business needs for the first few months.

"Okay," he calmly stated, looking over my paperwork. After he looked over my documents for a few seconds, he excused himself from the office. "Just a second. I will be right back," he said.

Although it had been years since I established a bank account, I knew his demeanor was a bit odd. But not wanting to jump to any conclusions, I chose to assume he was just in great need of a mandatory restroom break. However, after several minutes of silently sitting in his office, my initial suspicions were confirmed as he returned and denied me the bank account.

"I'm sorry, Mr. King. But your business isn't welcomed here at this time," he said.

I was completely shocked. I wasn't asking for a loan. I was merely looking for a bank to hold *my* money. I quickly left the bank in disgust.

Keep in mind, at the time; I was affiliated with White Jesus and the spirit of privilege. The spirit of privilege teaches one to rationalize the existence of any injustice, thus, making the victims the perpetrators. Because I had been exposed to and inundated with such a spirit, I too began to rationalize the injustice I just suffered.

"Why wasn't my business welcomed?" I asked myself. "Why couldn't I open a simple bank account? Clearly, it wasn't because I was black. Maybe they had a policy against *new* businesses. Sure. That's it. They don't allow new businesses," I thought. With that thought in mind, I went to a different branch of the same bank.

Going through the entire process again, I told the new bank officer of my intentions to open an account. He eagerly accepted my documents, my check and proceeded to open the bank account with no questions asked.

"Okay, Mr. King. All I need for you to do is to sign on the lines I have indicated," he said, handing me a stack of papers.

"I'm sorry, sir. I really appreciate you helping me and you being so kind. But I have decided not to do business with this bank," I said, as I placed my documents back into my portfolio and walked out. I didn't care what arguments White Jesus made, there was no way I would accept I wasn't a victim of racial discrimination. Although I lacked empathy for my black brothers and sisters, what I wanted most was someone to understand my plight and empathize with me. No matter how much I tried to wish them away, the struggles I faced as a black man were real and no amount of White Jesus could make me feel any different. I needed someone to talk to. I needed to express my frustration. And given the fact I had spiritually abandoned those who could understand my plight, there were only a few people in my spiritual network I could turn to—my fellow members of my White Jesus fraternity.

Shortly after the banking experience, I went to a small group Bible study sponsored by the white church I was attending. It wasn't my first time attending such a meeting. By now, I was pretty familiar with the members of the group, and they with me. I can't recall exactly what the group was discussing that particular evening, but I remember not being as interactive as I had been in the past. Nevertheless, I continued to listen to the lesson. As the meeting drew to a close, the session leader inquired if there was anything anyone wanted to discuss. Still bothered by my banking experience, I spoke up. I told the group how I was frustrated and struggling with making sense of the situation. I opened up about my feelings of resentment and anger. I explained how the gap between my Sunday worship experience and my Monday reality was causing me to be spiritually confused. I needed help. I wanted assistance. I required empathy.

Instead, several members of the group began making excuses for the banking officer. The rationalizations they gave were the same ones I initially created in my mind. "Perhaps, they had a policy against *new* businesses." No one wanted to call it what it was—discrimination. Others even began to tell personal stories about their experiences which clearly didn't apply. There was no encouragement to fight past the obstacles. I guess the encouraging messages were only reserved for Sunday mornings. There was no instruction to deal with my frustration and anger. There was no direction to overcome the confusion I was experiencing.

I left the meeting feeling more alone than when I came. I was convinced my time with White Jesus had run its course. Unfortunately, the one person who would understand (Black Jesus) would merely ignite the anger I was already feeling and wanted to do away with. While White Jesus explained away the truth of the struggle, Black Jesus ignited the fire and anger of the struggle. I wanted nothing to do with either of them. I simply needed to experience Jesus Christ—the same Jesus I read about in the Scriptures.

PART 3 – THE REVELATION

THE REALITY OF
RICKY BOBBY

O ne of my favorite movies is *Talladega Nights: The Ballad of Ricky Bobby,* featuring Will Ferrell and John Reilly. In the movie, Ricky Bobby (Ferrell) and his partner— Cal Naughton, Jr. (Reilly)—are top ranked NASCAR drivers competing to stay a part of NASCAR's elite. My favorite scene in the movie is when Ricky is praying over the family's dinner and specifically prays to *Baby Jesus.* The funniest part is after Ricky is chastised by several family members and reminded that Jesus was an adult, he still insists on praying to Baby Jesus because it's the Jesus he likes the best.

"I like the Christmas Jesus best and I'm saying grace," he comically tells his wife. "When you say grace, you can say it to grown up Jesus or teenage Jesus, or bearded Jesus, or who- ever you want," he says.

This conversation sparks a hilarious discussion around the dinner table of each person's favorite Jesus *character.* Although this is a scene from a movie and intended to make us laugh, reality doesn't seem to be too far from it.

While this book has focused on the divide between Black Jesus and White Jesus, the truth is many of us have created per- sonal images of Jesus based on our desires of what we want him to represent. For some, Jesus is a pillar of strength and power for a particular culture or race of people. Therefore, we get Black Jesus, White Jesus and even Hispanic Jesus. For others, Jesus is a supporter of their idealistic causes—hence, Liberal Jesus, Conservative Jesus, or even Homosexual Jesus. In the movie, Cal Naughton (Reilly) says, "I like to picture Jesus in a tuxedo t-shirt 'cuz it says I want to be formal, but I'm here to party too. 'Cuz I like to party so I want my Jesus to party."

Unfortunately, in an attempt to gain support for our personal agendas and causes, we have inadvertently taken what we would consider to be the best characteristics of any one or group of people and created our own personal Jesus.

For blacks, we focused on his power and fight for justice. We focused on redemption and his love for "the least of these" (Matt. 25:40), while highlighting certain physical attributes to draw lines of similarity to the African-American race. Whites have historically focused on his sovereignty while presenting Jesus as the perfect picture of a white citizen. They've operated with the assumption Jesus must be white because white culture teaches that all good things are...*white*. Conservatives leaned toward God's laws and judgment to drive their agenda, while liberals and homosexuals have been drawn to his grace. All of these are aspects of Jesus.

However, when singled out or inappropriately placed, they create distortions, leaving us with nothing more than a Mr. Potato Head Jesus. That is, a distorted image of Jesus (and God) with various characteristics pieced together. We then hold onto specific scriptural references to support the image we've created.

For example, growing up, I was under the impression if I did good things, God would *bless* me with what I wanted. In other words, if I were a good boy, I would get good things. This understanding paralleled my image of Santa Claus. Like Jesus, Santa Claus knew whether I was naughty or nice. If nice, I received his blessing with good gifts. To me, Jesus and Santa Claus were one and the same. However, as time went on, my image of Jesus transitioned from merely a Santa Claus-ish image to more of a genie. Scripture states, "If you ask anything in My name, that I will do (John 14:14)." Great. Leaning heavily on my misunderstanding of this scripture, I developed a list of wishes. My prayers consisted of a daily wish list of things I wanted God to deliver. More money. A nicer car. A great job, allowing me to get all the other things on my wish list.

As time continued, I learned about and accepted God as my Heavenly Father who loves me. Because I didn't have a solid relationship with my biological father and had minimal experience in understanding true fatherly love, I developed images around what this would mean to me, using various images of the perfect father I desired. At the time, *The Cosby Show* was an extremely popular television show. On this show, Bill Cosby played the prototypical father—Dr. Heathcliff Huxtable. Despite what many may feel of Bill Cosby's more recent troubles, his work through *The Cosby Show* inspired many people during this time. Dr. Huxtable was a devoted family man, loving husband and wise father. He was fun. Smart. Cool. And black. Dr. Huxtable's blackness attracted me because there was now a positive image I could attach myself to, someone who looked like me. It gave me hope. Dr. Huxtable provided me with the best image of a father. So, throughout much of my teenage years and adult life, my image of Jesus was composed of Santa Claus, a genie, and Dr. Huxtable, all wrapped up in one.

So, in many ways, I was very similar to Ricky Bobby. I created a personal image of Jesus and ran with it. I identified the characteristics I was fondest of and pieced them together to create a deity I could relate to and was proud to support. This was my Jesus.

In an earlier chapter, we discussed the *Personal Trinity* as the three primary components of every Christian believer. The Personal Trinity includes our personal theology, spiritual encounters, and physical experiences. Our personal theology is what we have come to understand and believe about God/Jesus.

Ideally, this component should be shaped by the Word of God, but in most cases, is shaped by other influences. If I am going to learn about someone, I would much rather learn from them. This is what God's Word is intended to do. It is our opportunity to learn about God from God. However, this is usually not the case, as this component is often influenced by our thoughts, ideas, issues, desires, experiences, and environments.

It is important to note that our personal theology is not our relationship with God. It is merely our understanding of God as influenced by others. Whether influenced by the Word of God or by outside variables, or both, our personal theology simply describes what we know *of* God. It is not an indication of our relationship or the degree of our potential relationship *with* God. It is our idea, image, or impression of God. It is similar to my personal idea (or perception) of my favorite person.

For example, one of my favorite actors is Denzel Washington. I can't say I've seen all of his movies. But I am sure I have seen a great deal of them as I've followed his career from his earlier acting days. From *Glory* to *Mo' Better Blues* to *Flight*, I attempted to watch every film he was remotely involved in. I even remember watching him as a kid in *A Soldier's Story* and in *St. Elsewhere*. Over the course of his career, I have admired his work and developed a particular perception of how he is in person. Although I don't have a personal relationship with him, I have a personal knowledge of him to such a degree that it helped me to develop an image of who he is. Because I have never encountered him in person, my perception could be and most likely is wrong. In fact, my perception may be so mis-aligned it may encourage the wrong behavior if I ever were to personally engage with him. This is how many of us have come to our personal theology. We've watched Jesus from afar through stories and others' depictions. We've watched others engage with him. We've simply learned about him through others. We've allowed others to tell his story without verifying the information for ourselves. We've gained a personal theology based on third-party information.

Another variable affecting our personal theology is our personal agenda. Earlier, I noted that while our personal theologies are to be influenced by the Word of God, they are often dictated by our thoughts, ideas, issues, desires, experiences and the environments we are engaged in. These things also affect the development of our personal agendas. Let's face it. All of us have some kind of relationship with God. It may be a very close relationship or a very distant one. Regardless of the degree of closeness, there is some sort of relationship that exists, along with a certain set of expectations of what we aim to receive from the relationship. If the relationship is a distant one, our expectations are few. However, if rather close, our expectations may be more defined and specific. Our personal agenda is the expectations we have of our relationship with God. The greatest difference between Black Jesus and White Jesus lies in the personal agendas of those who serve them.

For many black Christians, frustrations with struggle and strife influence a personal agenda of redemption. Struggles with poverty and financial hardship create expectations of prosperity and financial deliverance. Furthermore, a history of degradation creates a deep yearning for deliverance and salvation. Therefore, the personal agenda of blacks and followers of Black Jesus has always been to be saved, rescued and delivered. "Save me from my oppressors and my terrible circumstances!" they cry out. And since blacks can't possibly trust a white savior to save them from their white oppressors, they ensure their savior is coffee-colored.

On the other hand, whites have never desired or required salvation. What have they needed saving from, as they have historically enjoyed the top position on the social totem pole? Instead, their personal agenda has been to protect the position they've historically enjoyed. It is a position of power and privilege. What image helps them protect such a position? The image of Jesus as Lord. A lord is one who exercises authority over others. And he, of course, has to be a lord they can relate to. Thus, White Jesus takes on the role of the great white lord exercising and protecting the power, authority and privilege enjoyed by white Christians.

Unfortunately for whites, the last thing black Christians desire is another white lord, as this is the very thing they've sought salvation from. They don't want another master. Thus, blacks don't have a problem recognizing Jesus as savior. But Lord -- that's another story. On the other hand, whites don't have a problem with recognizing him as Lord. But savior? When have they needed one? Since Savior and Lord are both aspects of Jesus, the plausibility of Black Jesus and White Jesus begs little question. Married together, Savior and Lord are attributes that bring us into a world with no limitations. However, individually, they're crippling and create great discrepancies between our image and the actual image of Jesus Christ.

As we see, our personal agendas play a huge role in our personal image of Jesus and how we engage with him. However, this was never the initial intent. Again, our personal agendas are influenced by several outside factors. Our personal theology was never intended to be dictated by outside forces, but by the Word of God. We are to gain our understanding of God from God, Himself. This God-directed personal theology is to then influence our personal agendas. This is why the scripture says, "Delight yourself in the Lord; and He will give you the desires of your heart (Psalm 37:4 NASB)." Our personal agendas and desires are to be driven by our understanding and relationship with God.

As mentioned before, the components of the Personal Trinity are intended to support one another and have balance. So, our personal theology is to support our spiritual encounters and physical experiences. Our physical experiences are to support and be supported by both our personal theology and spiritual encounters. It's a spiritual check and balance system.

Now while our personal theology is the understanding that we have *of* God, it also serves as the foundation of our faith *in* God.

Romans chapter 10 says, "So faith comes by hearing, and hearing by the word of God (Romans 10:17)." Again, the Word of God is to drive our understanding of God and thus serve as the foundation of our faith *in* God. Working in conjunction with the Word of God, the Spirit of God brings us into encounters *with* God. Our encounters *with* God support our personal theology about God. They also aid in furthering our faith *in* Him. If our personal theology is limited, so will our spiritual encounters be. In Matthew 9:29, Jesus heals two blind men. Their personal agenda and theology were aligned as they recognized him for who he truly was. Thus, their faith served as the catalyst of their encounter with him. As they both requested healing, Jesus responds, "Do you believe that I am able to do this?" Their faith *in* him is the basis for their encounter *with* him as they say, "Yes." Jesus then heals them of their blindness, "according to their faith."

Our spiritual encounters with Jesus support our faith and also continue to build our faith. The more encounters we have with His Spirit, the greater our faith becomes. Lastly, our encounters *with* God affect how we respond to the people or things of God. This component is referred to as our physical experiences. When we encounter the Spirit of God, there is an impartation of His Spirit into our spirit. Therefore, the more we encounter His Spirit, the more we reflect Him. His Spirit then leads us in our daily dealings with others. Romans 8:14 says, "For as many as are led by the Spirit of God, these are the sons of God." It is the consistent leading of His Spirit, allowing us to be reflections of Him.

Notice the total transition taking place. The Word of God gives us a knowledge *of* God and builds our faith *in* God. Our faith *in* God is supported by our encounters *with* God. Our encounters *with* God lead us to greater reflection *of* Him. Our ultimate purpose is to reflect Him on Earth.

So, what does all of this have to do with Black Jesus and White Jesus? I am so glad you asked. I mentioned earlier Black Jesus and White Jesus are both born from fear. Black Jesus is born from a fear of never being saved and delivered. It's a fear of staying in bondage. White Jesus, on the other hand, is born from a fear of losing control and power. It's a fear of moving from independence to dependence. Again, it's a fear of bondage. Therefore, Black Jesus is known as savior and liberator while White Jesus is known as lord.

Because of this, blacks continue to seek salvation from their daily systemic struggles. If a savior is what is desired, there will only be a focus on situations in which a savior is relevant. Therefore, black Christians are inadvertently trained to highlight the struggle even though they've already been delivered from the struggle. There's such a fear of being in bondage that it's the only thing seen. It's the old adage that what you focus on is what you will perpetuate and receive. Black Christians focus so much on the struggle and fear of not being set free that they've missed the announcement of freedom.

In Texas, we celebrate a holiday called Juneteenth. Juneteenth is to commemorate the liberation of slaves on June 19, 1865, in Texas. Interestingly, while we acknowledge June 19, 1865 as the liberation date, slaves were freed a whole year in advance. However, the word had not reached the slaves in Texas. So, for an entire year they were still in bondage when the decree of their freedom had already been announced. This is similar to what the black Christian experiences. We have already been declared free in Christ, but for some reason, freedom hasn't been recognized by those still existing in bondage. So, they still cry out for a savior.

White Jesus, again, perpetuates privilege and thus seeks to maintain such privilege by demonstrating his lordship. This is driven by a fear of losing their power and independence Because there's such a fear of losing their privilege, privilege is perpetuated in the Church by suggestions of social and

economic privilege being tied to spiritual favor. The less fortunate are no longer victims of unfortunate circumstance or
systemic limitations, but they are perpetrators of their own sin
as they are the cause of their own misfortune. This is similar to
the story of Job. There's an understanding that if you are going
through unfortunate circumstances, it is a result of your sin. In
the book of Job, Job's friends were adamant about condemning
him for alleged sin against God because of his misfortune. Since
blacks' misfortune is prevalent throughout mainstream society,
it is understood that they don't rest in God's favor. They aren't
victims of a sinful social structure, but are sinful themselves.
They are, in many ways, cursed. With White Jesus, salvation
is not needed because privilege and power are already established. They have the power in education, business, science,
entertainment, and government. Because they have exercised
authority in these areas for so long, they have created a social
construct that exemplifies them as the standard. White becomes
right. Anything other than white must strive to purify and rid
itself of its proverbial stains. Therefore, blacks are conditioned
to assimilate to be accepted. White Jesus becomes the god of
success, self-indulgence, and self-edification.

This same attempt to protect is what leads many to volunteer
during the holiday season with little regard for those they're
to help, but merely to satisfy their own egos. Volunteering in
such fashion still demonstrates the line between those favored
at the top of the social totem pole versus those at the bottom. It
demonstrates a dependence by one group on the other, thereby
protecting the same feelings of power that exist. In turn, it also
allows the privileged to feel less guilty about their positions,
as it appears to help others rise to their current positions. It is
a spirit of false humility. Those worshipping White Jesus are
often in favor of the lines of demarcation between the "haves"
and the "have-nots" because it supports the notion that they're
better than the underserved.

Unfortunately, many Christians don't have a clue as to who they are aligned to. So, let me give you a few thoughts to help you discern where your allegiances might lie. For starters, it's important to note that although this book is primarily about the separation of races and cultures, these next thoughts will help expose your personal Jesus.

Secondly, you must also understand that your allegiance to Black Jesus or White Jesus is less about the color of your skin and more to do about a particular mindset and your personal agenda. So, there are many cases where non-blacks would be aligned to Black Jesus, and non-whites demonstrating allegiance to White Jesus. Others may find themselves in the middle. That is, they are in the process of crossing over from one to another.

Just as Ricky Bobby prayed to Baby Jesus, the discussion in this chapter lays the groundwork for you to discover your personal Jesus. There may be Conservative Jesus, Liberal Jesus, Romantic Relationship Jesus, Homosexual Jesus, to name a few. Your personal agenda will demonstrate who you are aligned with. Your personal agenda is often exposed in your prayer and worship life. What topics consume your prayer and worship life? Here are several questions suggesting an alignment to Black Jesus:

1. Are you constantly praying for deliverance from struggles?
2. Are you constantly praying for God to bring you into a new place financially?
3. Are you continuously feeling overwhelmed by life? Do you often feel like you will never get ahead?
4. When you worship, do you find yourself crying out to God for a break?
5. As a child, I would often hear my mother say, "If it ain't one thing, it's another." Does this describe how you feel about your life?

6. Do you have a tendency to act and speak about the past evils of whites and/or the government?
7. Are you consistently seeking cultural validation from biblical sources?
8. Do you often feel victimized by others in authority?

Again, these are just a few questions suggesting you may be aligned with Black Jesus. Remember, Black Jesus is often identified with the struggle of life. Those aligned with Black Jesus often seek salvation and a better way, while having little hope of any deliverance. They also often blame the establishment for their troubles. The following questions are indicative of those serving White Jesus:

1. What do you pray about most? Money? Job? Business? Opportunities? Open doors? Maintaining it all?
2. Do you often have ill feelings toward those on public assistance or the less fortunate?
3. Do you feel minorities' complaints of injustice are unwarranted? Do you feel they just need to get over it?
4. Do you prefer (or seek) to worship with those displaying affluence?
5. Does your Sunday worship time often take a back seat to recreational and extracurricular activities?
6. Can you name at least two people less fortunate than yourself who you can see yourself being mentored by? If not, it may be an indication of a lack of respect of those less fortunate, which is perpetuated with White Jesus.
7. What kind of charitable work do you engage in? Are there particular times of year where you typically perform charitable acts? If so, why do you typically engage in charitable works during this time of year?
8. Do people come to you more for money and networking or for prayer and guidance?

9. On a scale from 1 to 10 (least to most), how much validation/satisfaction do you receive when telling people about your job?

10. What steps are you taking to achieve your spiritual goals for this year? What steps are you taking to achieve your career/financial goals for this year? This particular question may highlight an imbalanced focus on climbing the socio-economic ladder.

THE P.E.D.I. CURE

The previous discussion of our personal Jesus is important because it indicates how effective we will be in our Christian mandate. In Matthew 28:18-20, Jesus gives his disciples what is commonly referred to as "The Great Commission." He says, "All authority has been given to me. [19] Therefore go and make disciples of all nations, baptizing them in the name of the Father and of the Son and of the Holy Spirit, [20] and teaching them to obey everything I have commanded you. And surely I am with you always, to the very end of the age (NIV)." At the foundation of what Jesus commanded was love. In Matthew 22:37-40, Jesus states the greatest commandments are to love God with all of our hearts and to love others. So, if I were going to restate the Great Commission, it would read, "Therefore go and make disciples of all nations...and teaching them to love — love God and others." Based on the mandate from Christ, we are to teach the world to love.

During my professional career, I spent several years as an adjunct business professor at two of Houston's local colleges. I can't remember a time in my youth where I sought to be a teacher. However, I always enjoyed teaching and leading others to greater truths. Teaching had become natural for me. So, when I needed a break from corporate America, I became a teacher. In my time as an instructor, I realized individuals learn differently. Some students, I could simply tell them what I wanted them to know and they would appear to immediately understand. Others, I needed to go into greater detail and explain the who, what, when, where, how and why of what I just told them. And then there was another group of students who needed to physically see what I was trying to teach. They were visual learners and needed to see the truths demonstrated in a practical way so they could understand how to apply the information themselves. Without the demonstration, they often missed the relevance of the information. Practical demonstration became the method I used to answer their questions of "What's the point?" and "How do I apply this in my world?" The same is the case in the Kingdom of God.

Christ calls us to make disciples of all nations. By definition, a disciple is a student who learns under the close supervision and authority of another. As his followers, Christ calls us to make disciples and teach the world what he taught us. Similar to teaching students in the classroom, there are several methods needed to ensure the world learns and understands how to apply Christ's teachings to their lives. When it came to discipleship, Jesus made disciples through his preaching and by his presence. That is, he preached and taught the gospel of the Kingdom along with allowing his actions to demonstrate what he taught. The preaching was not more important than the presence; nor the presence more important than the preaching. However, they both accompanied and supported one another.

I call these methods the **P.E.D.I. Cure**—Proclamation, Explanation, Demonstration and Illustration.

In Matthew chapter 4, when Jesus begins his earthly ministry, we see him teaching by "*proclaiming* the good news of the kingdom (Matthew 4:23 NIV)." Later in Matthew 13, we see Jesus teaching and *explaining* his lessons using parables so the people gain a better understanding of what is taught. Also throughout the Gospels, we see Jesus performing various miracles of compassion. Each miracle was performed out of the compassion and love he shared for the people. After healing many people for three days, Jesus says, "I have compassion on the multitude, because they have now continued with Me three days and have nothing to eat. And I do not want to send them away hungry, lest they faint on the way (Matthew 15:32)." Jesus then feeds more than 4,000 people with seven loaves of bread and a few small fish (with extras left over). Here, along with many other miracles, Jesus *demonstrates* the power and love he teaches. The proclamation, explanation and demonstration of His kingdom make way for the illustration of His kingdom. That is, for people of different backgrounds and histories to come together *in love* and worship God. Ultimately, as believers in Christ, we are to be able to proclaim, explain and demonstrate the gospel in such a way that it is reflected and illustrated in our lives, in our communities and throughout the nations. Simply put, segregation does not reflect the Kingdom of God. I admit I am not the greatest theologian in the world, but I have yet to find a scripture where Jesus is speaking of a black kingdom, white kingdom and so forth.

So far, the Church has done a pretty good job of preaching and proclaiming the Gospel of Jesus Christ. With constant technological improvements, proclaiming the gospel to the masses has become much easier than in decades past. Recently, the internet has given even the smallest ministries the ability to instantly reach people across the globe. Therefore, our ability to proclaim the gospel is not the problem. Although we haven't quite mastered the ability to explain the gospel, I would still give us a satisfactory mark in this area, as our collective understanding of the gospel has increased significantly over the past hundred years or so. However, when it comes to demonstrating the gospel of Jesus Christ, we have failed miserably.

We often hear of the miracles and healings Jesus performed. However, the foundation for all of the miracles that took place was the love and compassion he shared for the people. He didn't just have compassion for those who looked like him or for those who were of the same educational, religious, or even cultural background. As a matter of fact, Jesus healed those who his traditional Jewish roots would have suggested he not speak to (i.e., the leper, the centurion's servant and the bleeding woman, to name a few). These methods were not only used by Jesus, but also by the apostles of the early church.

Acts chapter 2 speaks of the early believers devoting "themselves to the apostles' *teaching*...Everyone was filled with awe at the *many wonders and signs performed by the apostles* (Acts 2:42-43, NIV, italics added)." Verse 47 goes on to say, "...the Lord added to their number daily..." Again, the early apostles followed the same model in discipleship they witnessed with Jesus. They consistently engaged in the proclamation, explanation and demonstration of the gospel, which allowed their communities to reflect and illustrate the unified Kingdom of God.

For some reason, God seems to lead me to people who aren't shy about expressing their frustration with the Church and their faith. Out of the many reasons I heard, there's one mentioned more than 80 percent of the time. That is, many people are frustrated and confused because they experienced a major disconnect between what they were taught versus what they experienced in the Church. They hear of love but rarely experience it. They're told they're welcomed, but instead are treated like outsiders. They hear of deliverance, but experience subjugation by the same people who preach freedom. They're told of miracles, but experience unanswered prayers. This is what blacks and other minorities experienced for many years. So collectively, the Church has had trouble demonstrating what's preached and explained.

Before we are able to witness change within our Christian communities, we first need to demonstrate love. It is through the love of God that the miracles of God can flow. If there is not love, there are no miracles. We see Jesus and the apostles first demonstrating love. In fact, I would venture to say the first miracle many of us will ever witness is experiencing the love of God in (and through) our lives. While it is our nature to desire love, it is not within our means to love as God loves. By nature we are drawn to those we share commonalities with. We gravitate to those like us, which breeds separation. We do not have the innate ability to truly love those who hurt us, who we differ from, or those we disagree with or don't understand. Therefore, for us to demonstrate a giving love to others as Christ commands, we must be led by God. Love is not just *of God*, but *God is Love*. And thus, love is God. Therefore, any word, action, or thing that is of God is based on His essence of love. Any time we are demonstrating love, we are allowing the Spirit of God to flow through us. 1 John 4:8 says, "He who does not love does not know God, for God is love."

A key word I want to bring your attention to in this passage is *know*. This word, as it's used in this passage, does not refer to an informational knowledge but speaks of an intimate knowledge through experience. So, this scripture is really saying, "Whoever does not love *has not experienced* God, because God is love." One cannot demonstrate what one doesn't *know* (or hasn't experienced). In Luke 3:22, we see Jesus' experience with the Spirit of God as the Holy Spirit descends upon him like a dove. Also in Acts 2, we see the apostles' experience with the Spirit of God at Pentecost. In both cases, the Spirit of God (Love) descends upon them. This experience empowers them in Love, which again is the pathway for signs, wonders and miracles to flow (or the demonstration of God's transformative power). The early church attracted people from all walks of life and all cultures. Interestingly enough, the cultural clashes witnessed during that time were far more intense than what we see today. Nevertheless, the love demonstrated broke down social, cultural and economic walls as the Christian communities began to illustrate and reflect the Kingdom of God. Many theologians and clergy have suggested the reason we've failed to see consistent miracles throughout the Church is due to a lack of faith. But it's not faith the Church lacks, it's Love. Love creates avenues for exciting things to happen and for changes to take place. And people are always drawn to exciting things taking place.

FROM THE ALTAR

When asked about my church roots, I often describe my childhood church experiences as being "Bapticostal," meaning I was heavily influenced by both Baptist and Pentecostal traditions. In the United States, Baptists and Pentecostals are the largest Protestant (non-Catholic) denominational Christian groups. It has been said there are more than 30,000 Christian denominations. The differences between each can typically be found in various doctrinal beliefs and styles of worship. Between Baptists and Pentecostals, a primary difference lies with their belief and practice of spiritual gifts (more specifically, speaking in tongues). Traditionally, Baptists do not acknowledge such charismatic gifts (speaking in tongues, healings, prophecy, and miracles, to name a few) as being relevant for today. For a list of these charismatic gifts, see 1 Corinthians 12:4-11.

As a Baptist church, we held true to traditional Baptist teachings. So, I was rarely exposed to such gifts being freely practiced in our worship services. However, as a black church, aspects of Pentecostalism (particularly worship styles) would often find their way into our worship services. As noted before, Pentecostalism greatly influenced the black church as aspects of the Pentecostal worship experience became closely fused into black culture. Regardless of my church roots, there was

140

one aspect of many worship services, whether in predominantly white or black congregations, that was pretty consistent. That was the altar call.

The altar call is the period after the preacher's sermon in which an appeal is made for sinners to publicly receive salvation. Oftentimes, the altar call involves an emotional plea by the pastor to encourage the so-called sinner to walk down the aisles of the church to accept Jesus Christ as their Lord and Savior. Sometimes the plea would even include fear tactics. "If you died tonight and you don't know if you would go to heaven or hell, you should come right now to the altar," pastors would say. I admit, that speech got me to the altar several times. It literally scared the *hell* out of me.

Over the years, this practice has been known by many names and has taken many forms. Initially called the altar call, it was later referred to as the public invitation to discipleship. Growing up, my pastor would stand atop the pulpit and say, "The doors of the church are now open," indicating it was the time when one should come to the altar, repenting of their sins, give their life to Jesus Christ and join the church. The altar call was intended to be the most respected time of the worship service. All movement of the members would cease. The ushers would all but barricade the doors to keep members from leaving the sanctuary (auditorium). The only noise to be heard would be the sound of the pastor's voice, accompanied by the choir singing in the background. While I completely understand the importance of the altar call during the worship service and to the overarching goal of the Church, I also believe it served as a great limitation in the Church's ability to demonstrate the unity Christ prayed for in John 17.

Altar calls first gained popularity in the early 1800s as a method to determine how many, and which people were actually converted after hearing a preacher's message. Upon hearing the gospel message, every person is faced with a choice—to receive or reject the message. I understand the altar call brings that choice to the forefront. However, based on my under-standing of the members of the first century church, I can't dare subscribe to the belief that altar calls were the intended end result that they have become in today's modern church. I have no plans to argue for or against the use of altar calls. As I have stated before, I do recognize their benefit. However, through a close examination of the altar, we will see there's much more to what God intended with the salvific experience that many of us have not tapped into. It's the *more* that is the key to breaking the racial, generational, gender, economic and cultural barriers we have perpetuated within the Church. However, to understand the limitations of the altar call, we must first look back at the intent of the altar in the Old Testament.

In Genesis 2:15-17, God places Adam in the garden of Eden and gives him his marching orders—to tend and keep the garden. Along with his directions, God also gives Adam the parameters he must adhere to and the consequences if those parameters are not followed. "Of every tree of the garden you may freely eat; but of the tree of the knowledge of good and evil you shall not eat, for in the day that you eat of it, you shall surely die." Most of us know what later happens in this story. Adam and his wife disobey God's parameters and they're punished. What does this have to do with the altar of the Old Testament? I'm glad you asked.

In Genesis 3:14, God begins enforcing consequences for their disobedience. Although God told Adam he would die for violation of His orders, we see neither Adam nor Eve suffered a physical death. If they had, I am pretty sure the Bible would be a lot shorter. We are most interested in what happens in verse 21, "Also for Adam and his wife the Lord God made tunics of skin, and clothed them." In this passage, we see two key prin ciples established. The first is the principle of grace and atone ment. In this passage, we see the first implication of an animal sacrifice. An animal sacrifice was performed by God on behalf of Adam and Eve. Here, God graciously establishes a method of atonement by substituting the life (blood) of an animal for the life of man. According to God's law, sin required death (Rom. 6:23). However, the death sacrifice of an animal would serve as a substitutionary death that was due to the sinner, thus restoring them back to right relationship with God. This system of sacrifice would later be pivotal in Israel's relationship and experience with God.

The second principle we see is God replacing the self-made righteousness of Adam and Eve with His own—the tunic. The tunic of animal skin (which was made from the sacrifice) was used to replace the fig leaves Adam and Eve had sewn together to cover themselves. Those coverings were used to cover their guilt and shame and thus, were not sufficient. Therefore, God provides a covering for them through the sacrifice. The replacement of self-righteousness with God's righteousness would later be important for God's people.

The point of all of this is to understand that it is at the altar where all of this takes place—the atoning sacrifice and God's righteousness. In the Old Testament, Israel's experience with God would include them building an altar and offering an animal sacrifice. The animal sacrifice would serve as a replacement to the death that was due to the one who sinned, thus restoring him to a right relationship with God. In their sacrifice, they were recognizing who God was and who He was *to them*. It was an act of worship, reverence, and repentance. However, after their exodus from Egypt, the Israelites were instructed by God to build the Tabernacle. The Tabernacle would become the central place of worship and sacrifice while the Israelites were in the wilderness.[28] After their time in the wilderness, they would later recreate the Tabernacle as their temple in Jerusalem. Just stick with me, there's a point to all of this.

The Tabernacle was divided into three primary areas—the outer court, the inner court (or Holy Place), and the Holy of Holies (or Most Holy Place). The outer court was where most of the people would convene. It was also the place where the people would bring animals to be sacrificed for their particular sins. The sacrifices would be burned on the brazen *altar* in the outer court. The inner court would be where the priests would function. It was the priests' role to offer the animals brought as sacrifices to God on behalf of the people. During this process, the priests would examine the sacrifice brought to ensure it was unblemished and suitable to be offered to God. The person making the sacrifice would place their hand on the head of the animal. This was an act to identify with the sacrifice and thus transfer the sinner's sins to the animal. At that point, the priests would kill the animal and sprinkle its blood around the sanctuary and on the altar.

The Holy of Holies was where the glory of God dwelt. It was the most sacred place of the Tabernacle, separated by a large veil, and only the high priest would enter. One day out of the year—Yom Kippur (the Day of Atonement)—the high priest would enter into the Holy of Holies to atone for the sins of the nation. Prior to entering, the high priest would cleanse himself; wear special clothing and burn incense, in an effort to recognize God's holiness. The high priest was the only one to go beyond the veil on behalf of the people. The veil separated man from God and served as a reminder that no one could irreverently enter into God's presence. However, Jesus' death removed the veil.

Jesus' death was both a sacrificial and vicarious death. He sacrificed his life for you and me and became the sacrifice for us all. He experienced a death that should have been assigned to us. How could this be the case? In John 1:29, we first see Jesus introduced by John the Baptist as "the Lamb of God who takes away the sins of the world." Here, John makes a reference to the old sacrificial system of animal sacrifice. Being without sin, Jesus was unblemished and thus capable of being a sacrifice for us. Therefore, the cross of Christ represents the altar on which his blood was sprinkled and poured for our sins.

Also, when Christ died, the veil separating the Most Holy Place from the rest of the temple in Jerusalem was literally torn from top to bottom. Remember, it was in the Most Holy Place where God's presence rested. Therefore, upon Christ's death, God's presence was available to all. No longer would we be required to offer animal sacrifices to have a restored relationship with God. Also, no longer would the presence of God be restricted to only the high priest. Jesus became our high priest. "This hope we have as an anchor of the soul, both sure and steadfast, and which enters the Presence behind the veil, where the forerunner has entered for us, even Jesus, having become High Priest forever according to the order of Melchizedek (Hebrews 6:19-20)."

So, in both the Old and New Testaments, the sinner would repent at the altar, demonstrate reverence and be restored. Even in today's altar calls, the expectation is that the sinner is publicly repenting of their sins and their sinful state. They are also publicly declaring their reverence for God (and Jesus Christ). That is a declaration of who He is (in His sovereignty), what He has done (in His sacrifice) and who He is to them—Lord and Savior. So, if the expectations of today's altar call align with what the altar symbolized in Hebraic times, what's the issue? Where's the limitation?

If you recall, we said upon Christ's death, the veil tore, making God's presence available to all. But why? The tearing of the veil was not only a removal of a barrier between God and man, but was also an invitation for man to now experience the presence of God through Jesus Christ. There was an indication and an invitation. Remember the veil was what separated the Most Holy Place from the other places of the Tabernacle. As the high priest entered the Most Holy Place, he was able to experience the glory of God in much greater capacity than any others. The high priest had the privilege of experiencing God's presence. The tearing of the veil indicated we were now able to have a new experience in God and also invited us to do so.

> Therefore, brothers and sisters, since we have *confidence to enter the Most Holy Place by the blood of Jesus*, [20] by a new and living way opened for us through the curtain, that is, his body, [21] *let us draw near to God* with a sincere heart and with full assurance that faith brings...
> (Hebrews 10:19-22 NIV)

In this passage, there are two places I want to highlight. I added italics for emphasis. First, the writer of Hebrews reiterates our access to the Most Holy Place and the presence of God through Jesus Christ. Second, there's an appeal (or a call) inviting us to draw near to God in intimacy. A paraphrase of this passage would read, "Because we are assured entry into the Most Holy Place, let's go experience God's presence and a relationship with Him." Indirectly, this passage also contrasts our previous capabilities (or lack thereof) of experiencing God. "Before, we couldn't; but now we can. And since we can; let's progress toward an intimate experience with God." This means there is something greater taking place behind the veil. There is more in His presence than there is at the altar. This difference is the key to breaking down the barriers existing between White Jesus and Black Jesus.

As we noted earlier, the altar was and still is a place of repentance, reverence and restoration. So, when one publicly answers the pastor's altar call, it is expected and understood that they are repentant of their sinful life. They are paying reverence to God for who He is and what He has done through His Son Jesus Christ, and they are being restored into a right-standing relationship with God. But as we also noted, in the Tabernacle, the altar was located in the outer court, which one would encounter prior to the Most Holy Place. In fact, before one would have the opportunity to enter the Most Holy Place they would have to go through the outer court or come to the altar. Plainly put, this shows that after Jesus died, the altar was not the end goal. It was merely the means to get to the end, which was the presence of God. So, even in today's context, our focus on simply leading people to the altar is to mistake the means for the end. It's the same as a taxi driver picking you up and dropping you off halfway to your intended destination. Instead of acknowledging you are only partially to your destination, the taxi driver tries their best to convince you this is exactly where you are supposed to be.

Another shortfall of today's altar call is that it does not address the garbage often brought for disposal. Over the course of my life, I have seen thousands of people accept the pastor's invitation to the altar. Each person I watched come to the altar has come with more than a repentant heart. They come with bags of garbage. I am referring to the garbage of guilt, shame, despair, fear, their insecurities, and so on. Oftentimes, these feelings are weighing so heavy on the person you can see the effects on their body. So, the weight of their burdens is so heavy it compels them to come to the altar. Once at the altar, they lay down their bag of garbage, repent, recognize God, and get spiritually restored unto God, only to pick up their bag of emotional garbage and return to their previous state.

But it's in the presence of God where transformation takes place. However, as we see in the Tabernacle, to experience the presence of God, one must go *through* the altar, as opposed to simply going *to* the altar. Therefore, our aim should not be to simply lead people to the altar, but to an authentic experience with God's presence. Now we understand the altar is the *means* to His presence. However, there are two additional questions that come to mind: 1) what happens in His presence? And 2) what does this have to do with the various cultural lines we see in the Church?

When you experience God, you also get a glimpse of His essence, which is love. So many people think God is some mean, tyrannical being sitting high on a mountaintop, waiting to destroy them with lightning bolts every time they do something wrong. This is so far from the truth. I admit, growing up, this was my idea of God. This was the same theological understanding I possessed as an eight-year-old boy. But, God's nature is love. Everything about Him is based on His essence of love. I can safely and confidently say anyone still seeing God as a mean tyrant has not experienced Him. There's no way to experience God and not experience His love.

In fact, God's nature is the one thing we go through our lives seeking. Regardless of race, culture, sex, age, or economic status, we all have an innate desire and need to experience love. Well, this is God. He is love. "And we have known and believed the love that God has for us. God is love, and he who abides in love abides in God, and God in him (1 John 4:16)." So, when you go from the altar to His presence, the primary thing you will experience is His love. Despite what you may have done in your life. Remember, your sins were atoned for and washed away at the altar of the cross. Therefore in His presence, your only responsibility is to enjoy Him and His love. This love becomes the basis of your change and the transformation of the Church.

The wonderful thing about God's presence is that it is revealing. God is love and His love is His light. It is the purest light. Scripture says while God is love, He is also light (1 John 1:5-7). His light reveals we aren't as holy as we may think. In God's presence, you clearly recognize how blemished you are. How is this a wonderful thing? Well, in the revelation of how blemished you are, you also experience His grace and mercy. That is, no matter how blemished and fallible you may be, He still loves and wants a relationship with you. Also, in His presence you witness how He sees you after you have been washed and cleansed of your sins. This is the beauty of His presence.

For illustration purposes, imagine yourself playing in a muddy park during a thunderstorm. You (and everyone else) play for hours and are covered with mud. Since everyone else is covered with mud, you don't recognize the degree of your filthiness until you go home. You travel home, which is painted the purest of white, including furnishings and decorations. Even your Father is adorned in the purest of white. At that moment, you realize how dirty you are. But instead of kicking you out for bringing mud into His house, He washes you, extends His arms in love and tells you that you never have to play in mud again. He then tells you how special you are and wants you to bring other muddy people to His house so they also can be cleaned.

Although very simplified, this is how it is when we experience God. Despite the dirt we've accumulated, He washed us and shows us who we are to Him. In that experience, we are to see ourselves (and others) through His eyes. Regardless of the differences, regardless of the perceived dirt. We are valuable. We are cherished. We are loved in the eyes of God. God's eyes do not see cultural, racial, economic, or generational differences. In fact, to separate His children by such differences is as crazy as to separate them by eye color. By maintaining divisions, we are not abiding in love. His love is *experienced* in His presence in the Most Holy Place. My suggestion for the Church is to move past the altar into His presence. As we seek His presence and continue to be led by Him, it changes our perspective of our differences.

U-N-I-T-Y

I n the book, *United by Faith: The Multiracial Congregation As an Answer to the Problem of Race*, the authors make the argument that when possible, Christian churches should be multiracial. The authors cite that of the many Christian congregations in the United States, only a little more than 5 percent are multiracial. This is where no one racial group makes up 80 percent or more of the congregation.[29] And while I can honestly say at the time of this writing that our own church congregation has not met this mark, it is the Church's responsibility to lead the charge to break down the barriers of the racial divide in the world.

I've mentioned earlier that the Church perpetuated racism through its practices and propaganda. This is not just the case with white Christians, but with blacks and other cultural groups as well. This is also not just seen through their practices and teachings. While many will never physically state a preference for cultural segregation, there are many within the Church who overtly argued for its continuation. In *United by Faith* the authors cite several reasons discovered from their research for the continuation of racial segregation in the Church. A key argument given is that racial and cultural segregation provides comfort and safety for the congregants while providing cultural affirmation in a spiritual environment. The only problem is that this sounds extremely hypocritical, as it encourages us to cry about racial and cultural injustices in the world while evangelizing similar injustices in our churches. There's something about that that just doesn't make sense to me. More importantly, it's totally contrary to what Jesus desired of us. I will even go further to say anyone who perpetuates segregation is not led by the Spirit of God. In fact, this is not of Christ, but of anti-Christ. Let's look at Jesus' prayer for unity. His prayer in John chapter 17 gives us insight into his desire for future believers.

> [20] I do not ask on behalf of these alone, but for those also who believe in Me through their word; [21] that they may all be *one* (italics added); even as You, Father, are in me and I in you, that they also may be in Us, so that the world may believe that You sent Me. [22] The glory which You have given Me I have given to them, that they may be *one*, just as We are *one*; [23] I in them and You in me, that they may be perfected in *unity*, so that the world may know that You sent Me, and loved them, even as You have loved Me (John 17:20-23, NASB).

In this passage, Jesus doesn't reserve his prayer for his closest disciples, but for everyone who comes to knowledge and belief in him through the preaching of the gospel. This includes you and me. His prayer is for unity of the believers. I believe he focuses on unity for two reasons: 1) He knows we need it to successfully overcome the influence of the world; and 2) He knows the world needs us to have it. No one is as effective as they could be by themselves. There are several old adages that express this thought. "Two is better than one." "There's strength in numbers." We also see unity displayed in nature when animals graze, hunt and commune. Individuality expands one's vulnerability. In his prayer, Jesus wants us to understand that for us to withstand the wiles of the enemy and this world, we will need to be unified. If not, we leave ourselves vulnerable to be overtaken by "Satan's devices."[30] Secondly, he prays for unity because it's the only way the world will experience God's love and thus come to a knowledge of and belief in Him.

Jesus prays for believers to be united as he and the Father are united. It's important we know the bond connecting Jesus with the Father is the bond of the Father's Spirit. That's right, the Holy Spirit. The same Holy Spirit now lives within us as believers. This is the perfect union—Father, Son and Holy Spirit. So, Jesus prays for this indwelling of the Holy Spirit to have the same role in lives of believers as in him, which is to unify believers from different cultures, economic classes, genders and so forth.

During this time, believers in Jesus Christ were few when compared to the rest of society. They were definitely a minority and many times, experienced persecution. So, regardless of the skin color or particular culture where one may have originated, the bond of being a believer in Christ alone brought them together. There's something about being able to relate to another's experiences that strengthens the bond between you. It's the very reason teammates on an athletic team can be so close, yet so different. It's the same reason homosexuals can find strength in their particular communities. And it's the exact same reason black people give each other nods of solidarity when in predominantly white environments. There's not only strength in numbers, but there's strength found in the struggle. And when people can relate and have respect for one another's struggles, there's just a natural bond that brings them together.

This is the bond first century Christians would have experienced. This is the bond that would have initially connected them. But while this similarity would serve as an initial bond, it wasn't sufficient enough to achieve the ultimate vision, which was to bring the world to a knowledge and belief in Jesus Christ.

152

While the Spirit of God would serve as the catalyst for believers to be united with one another, He would also serve as the unifying bond to Father and Son, allowing the believer to experience the perfect union characterized by love.

There are three things Jesus hopes to accomplish through our unity: 1) for the world to know the Father *sent* him; 2) for them to know the Father *loved* them; and 3) for them to be *filled* with that same love.

We see in this passage, Jesus desires for the world to know he was sent by the Father. That he is the Christ, the Messiah, sent by God. Something interesting takes place in this dialogue between the Father and Son. In John 17:21, Jesus indicates his desire for unity is "so that the world may *believe* that You sent Me." The word *believe* is expressed by the Greek word meaning to trust, believe, or have confidence in. This is the same word used when we talk about faith. It's the same word used in Romans 10:9 when Paul explains our salvation. In his prayer, Jesus desires the unity of believers so the world may trust, or have faith (confidence) in not only the fact that God sent him, but also in God's purpose and involvement in his death, burial and resurrection. This is to take place as a result of the believers' unity in the gospel message.

In verse 23, we see a progression from the previous thought. Here, Jesus says he prays for us to be "perfected in unity, so that the world may *know* that You sent Me, and loved them." If you recall earlier (in the verse), he wants the world to simply believe the Father sent him. Now, I don't want to minimize the notion of one's belief that Jesus is the Messiah. However, I want to point out there is something greater taking place here. Again, the word *know* is more than a rational knowledge one may attain from books. It is also more than a mere knowledge of something. This word indicates an intimate knowledge through relations(hip). That's right, it indicates a knowledge gained through intimate relations. So, Jesus is saying he desires believers to be united to one another and unto him so the rest of the world can come to an experiential knowledge of God. Jesus desires that we know Him not just in theory, but in intimate experience. Through this experience, the world will realize he was sent by the Father because the Father loved them. Notice, Jesus doesn't just call for us to be united, but he calls for our *perfection* in unity. Contrary to what many may think or even teach, this word *perfect* has nothing to do with our ability to attain ultimate morality and successfully fulfill a list of "thou shalt nots." However, this word suggests completeness, maturity and being undivided. As I stated before, the perfect union can be witnessed in the bond between the Father, Son and Holy Spirit. Here, Jesus is calling for us to experience, through the Holy Spirit, the perfect union between himself and the Father.

I also noted earlier, there is a certain progression that takes place in this dialogue. Let's continue to verse 26. Jesus states, "...so that the love with which You loved Me may be in them, and I in them." Jesus prays for our unity so the world can believe or have faith in him. This belief is the road unto salvation. But wait; there's more. Upon this belief, the world will not only believe God sent Jesus, but they will also *know* the reason he was sent—love. This belief comes from the proclamation of the gospel message and with the leading of the Holy Spirit. Jesus says he wants the world to come to a further experiential knowledge of God. Again, this is an intimate, relational knowledge that occurs through the Holy Spirit with the intention to have another result.

In other words, God seeks to have an experience with us to birth something else out of us. Through this experience, Jesus desires we not just know of God's love, but that it resides in us. This is not simply a love present at certain times within us but it is a complete filling of love. It should be filled, so much so that love pours out of us. The aim is for us to have an over flow of love. And as we possess this overflow, those we come into contact with will be affected by that same overflow of love. That which is in us will flow or be birthed out of us. Thus, if we are united in love, the same love within us will be birthed into the world through us. This unity is to be with all believers. The Church is to be a vessel for love to pour out to all cultures. So, Jesus prays for us to have unity based on love. He understands whatever serves as the foundation of this unity will be perpetuated in all other relationships and dealings. This is our Lord's prayer.

Earlier, I mentioned there are many within the Church who have overtly argued for continued segregation among Christian congregations, therefore, perpetuating an anti-Christ spirit. I understand that's a very strong statement to make. However, division is the exact antithesis of what Christ prayed for and desired for believers. If it is in direct contrast with what Christ prayed for and was about, it is anti-Christ. There is no way one can be aligned with the mission and vision of Christ and support such practices. Christ prayed for unity, not division based on the color of one's skin or cultural background. To create competing doctrinal practices contradicting the Word of God, for the sake of cultural affirmation and comfort, is to place our will above God's.

Christ prayed so we would be united across the cultural and social lines the world has established. We are to be united in love and called to one mission. The love we experience is to overcome the minute differences of culture and class. To allow these differences to separate us in our mission is to love the differences more than we love Christ. It's the breaking down of these differences and the unification in mission that will begin to change the world. If we want to see a change in race relations and cultural tensions, let's be the change within the Church.

I HAVE A DREAM

On August 28, 1963, Martin Luther King, Jr., delivered his famous "I Have a Dream" speech in Washington, D.C., which called for an end to racial injustice across the country. This speech is arguably one of the greatest speeches of American and world history. In it, King provides hope by describing a better day when all people can join hands in harmony. And while it was extremely pivotal in rallying blacks across the country, I believe we are still missing something from the better day King described. I know I run the risk of being stoned and possibly losing my "black card" for saying this, but I believe King's speech was less about blacks and their rights, and more about the vision God gave him. Let me explain.

Dr. King's dream was a dream in which love prevailed. Remember, love unifies; fear divides. He saw a world where people could come together in love. Because this was the unifying force, his call to blacks during oppression was to love. He understood white America was driven by fear. But if blacks were to respond with fear and anger, no progress would be made. Anger does not combat fear, but only adds to it. Again, love combats fear. I believe his aim was to encourage blacks to pour out the love they have for one another onto their oppressors. Dr. King understood that for the Kingdom's vision to be manifested, it must begin with blacks responding to their enemies with love. This love would hopefully overcome the hatred of white America. Blacks weren't going to attain equal rights and social significance by force. Equal rights would only be obtained when blacks were viewed with equal value, which in turn, could only be realized if whites saw them through the loving eyes of God.

Therefore, I believe Dr. King's mandate was less about the equal rights of blacks and more about God's kingdom being reflected. However, the oppressive treatment of blacks was more of a roadblock for that vision to manifest. Since it was a major roadblock, it became the opportunity and platform to bring to awareness God's vision. At the time of this writing, it has been fifty-three years since Dr. King's famous speech, and his dream has yet to become a reality. But as God has shown me, there's more to that dream.

September 1997 was one of the toughest months of my entire life. My mother suddenly passed away from a brain aneurysm. While the details are less important, the weeks following sent me spiraling into a depressed trance. I was in my third year at Drake University and took the loss extremely hard. I was a train wreck waiting to happen. My vicious mood swings took my friends and loved ones on such a roller coaster ride, it's a miracle they didn't give up on me. Attempting to drown my sorrow, I bathed my kidneys in as much alcohol as I could get my hands on. With each passing day, I continued to lose myself in the sea of despair until I no longer knew who I was. I was on a downward spiral to nowhere, teetering on the edge of the point of no return.

At this point, there were only two people who could possibly help me—my mother, who was deceased, and God, who I blamed. The loneliness, the desolation and despair became too much for me to bear. The mere thought of continuing with my life seemed pointless as I began to contemplate options to end it all. While suicidal thoughts weighed me down, the truth is, I didn't have it in me to carry out such a task. In my desperation, I merely cried out to God to end my life.

During this time, I often cried myself to sleep, questioning God about my life. One night after one of my prayerful cries, God met me and showed me a vision I will never forget. After being asleep for what could have been several hours, I heard God's voice.

"I've heard you," the voice said. It was a calm, peaceful voice, much like the voice of a loving father calmly speaking to a child. God was actually speaking to me. "Your mother is fine. It was her time. She did everything she was supposed to do. She labored long and hard. It's time for her to come home," He assured me.

Up until that point, I failed to gain closure of my mother's death, as I never spoke to her prior to her departure. So, God's assurance was needed for me to be able to move forward.

As the conversation continued, God said, "It's not your time now. What I have given you, you are to impact many lives. But you must make the decision to follow me."

As He said this, I could see the faces of my two brothers, along with thousands of others. I saw white, black and brown faces. I saw people of all shapes, colors and ages. I saw the lonely, the hopeless and the lost. I saw the rich and the poor all gathered together. It was as if they all were looking up to the heavens. I saw hundreds of thousands, perhaps millions of people gathered, singing one beautiful worship song to God. While not everyone spoke the same language, the worship sounded unified. But this wasn't just restricted to the United States. This unified worship was happening simultaneously in the four corners of the globe. It was one worship. One sound unto God. God was showing me The Dream. And in showing me The Dream, He was calling me to a life of purpose. His dream became my dream. And almost twenty years later, fifty-three years after Dr. King delivered his famous speech, I am telling the world, "I have a dream."

I have a dream where the Church is united in Love, producing loving families, loving communities and loving nations.

I have a dream of a culture of old white men embracing young black men, praying and worshipping in love.

I have a dream. Not one in which the black church forcefully integrates with the white church for improved public relations during social chaos, but a church where there is no distinction between black or white.

I have a dream where we no longer ignore the current and historical systems of privilege and degradation, but one in which they are acknowledged, and through love, together we cry out to Jesus as Savior and Lord.

I have a dream in which fear is no longer the driving force, and when fear arises, it is combated with God's perfect love.

I have a dream where differences are appreciated, but unity is the choice.

I have a dream where cultures and generations will together accept the invitation to the Most Holy Place and the steel curtain of racism is torn, as the veil was torn in the tabernacle upon Jesus' death.

I have a dream where blacks, whites, Asians and Hispanics, rich, poor, men, women and children all over the world are revived to significance without demonizing the others.

I have a dream of us all standing arm in arm crying in each of our native tongues, "Hallelujah to the Most High God!" As our cry ascends to the heavens, it creates one heavenly sound we all hear and understand.

I have a dream where love rules and reigns in the hearts of men all over the earth. And in doing so, we will be led from our isolated temples of Black Jesus and White Jesus to experience the true unifying love of Jesus Christ.

I have a dream—God's dream—of one people, one worship, and one glorious sound. In Jesus' name. Amen.

END NOTES

[1] Edwards, Paul. "Sunday at 11: 'The Most Segregated Hour in This Nation'." *God & Culture,* http://www.godandculture. com/blog/sunday-at-11-the-most-segregated-hour-in-this-nation. Accessed 24 July 2016.

[2] Alexander, Estrelda, and Albert George Miller. "Introduction." *The Black Fire Reader: A Documentary Resource on African American Pentecostalism.* Eugene, OR: Cascade, 2013. N. pag. Print.

[3] Ibid.

[4] Ibid.

[5] See Three-Fifths Compromise of 1787.

[6] "Population Estimates, July 1, 2015, (V2015)." *Iowa QuickFacts from the US Census Bureau.* The United States Census Bureau, n.d. Web. http://www.census.gov/quick-facts/table/PST045215/19. Accessed 12 Sept 2016.

[7] Harrison, Bob. *When God Was Black.* Canoga Park, CA: Bob Harrison Ministries International, 1978. 154. Print.

[8] "Racial Attitudes of Blacks in Multiracial Congregations Resemble Those of Whites, Study Finds." *Media Communications | Baylor University.* Baylor University,

17 Aug. 2015. Web. http://www.baylor.edu/mediacommu-nications/news.php?action=story&story=159118. Accessed 05 Sept 2016.

⁹ Ibid.

¹⁰ Ibid.

¹¹ Harrison 159.

¹² Alexander loc. 3140.

¹³ Ibid. loc. 234.

¹⁴ Ibid.

¹⁵ Synan, Vinson. "The Pentecostal Century: An Overview." *The Century of the Holy Spirit 100 Years of Pentecostal and Charismatic Renewal, 1901-2001*. Nashville: Thomas Nelson, 2012. 1-9. Print.

¹⁶ Blake, Jon. "Black preachers who 'whoop'—minstrels or ministers?" *CNN.com*, http://www.cnn.com/2010/LIVING/10/20/whooping/index.html. Accessed 07 Oct 2016.

¹⁷ Alexander loc. 274.

¹⁸ Blake.

¹⁹ Alexander.

²⁰ Smith, James E. *The Pentateuch*. 2nd ed. Old Testament Survey Series. Joplin, MO: College Press Pub. Co., 1993.

²¹ Turner, John G. "Why Race Is Still a Problem for Mormons. *The New York Times*. The New York Times, 18 Aug 2012. Web. http://www.nytimes.com/2012/08/19/opinion sunday/racism-and-the-mormon-church.html. Accessed 0 Oct 2016.

22 Walker, Jade. "Interracial Marriage In The U.S. Climbs To New High, Study Finds." *The Huffington Post*. TheHuffingtonPost.com, 16 Feb. 2012. Web. http://www.huffingtonpost.com/2012/02/16/interracial-marriage-in-us_n_1281229.html. Accessed 20 May 2015.

23 Pew Research Center, March, 2014, "Millennials in Adulthood: Detached from Institutions, Networked with Friends" p.42.

24 Gallup, Inc. "In U.S., 87% Approve of Black-White Marriage, vs. 4% in 1958." *Gallup.com*. Gallup Inc, 25 July 2013. Web. http://www.gallup.com/poll/163697/approve-marriage-blacks-whites.aspx. Accessed May-June 2015.

25 Wang, Wendy. Pew Research Center, February, 2012, "The Rise of Intermarriage: Rates, Characteristics Vary by Race and Gender" p.7.

26 Synan.

27 Ibid.

28 http://the-tabernacle-place.com/articles/what_is_the_tabernacle/

29 DeYoung, Curtiss Paul. *United by Faith: The Multiracial Congregation as an Answer to the Problem of Race*. New York: Oxford UP, 2004. Print.p.1.

30 2 Corinthians 2:11

CPSIA information can be obtained
at www.ICGtesting.com
Printed in the USA
BVOW07s1044151017
497717BV00008B/192/P